'A new approach to economics is needed to tackle grotesque inequalities of wealth and power. Community Wealth Building offers a way for communities to confront corporate power and build a more equal and democratic economy. In this book Joe Guinan and Martin O'Neill show what inspiring action is already happening on the ground and point beyond to what is possible.'

Jeremy Corbyn MP, Leader of the Labour Party

'Change is coming, and another world is not just possible but already within reach. Joe Guinan and Martin O'Neill show how Community Wealth Building approaches can allow every community in the country to play their part in building a new economy from the ground up.'

John McDonnell MP, Shadow Chancellor of the Exchequer

'Joe Guinan and Martin O'Neill present a compelling vision of a more just, democratic economy in which wealth and power are more fairly shared. This book should be read by anyone who believes that a different economic order is possible and wants to know how we start to make it happen.'

Ed Miliband, MP for Doncaster North and former Leader of the Labour Party

'If you want to make the city where you live more equal and more democratic, this is the book for you. It shows what local government, institutions, and people can do to create a better world – even without the support of central government. It is at once both practical and inspiring.'

Richard Wilkinson and Kate Pickett, authors of *The Spirit Level* and *The Inner Level*

'*The Case for Community Wealth Building* is an essential guide to a new and devolved economic movement that challenges forty years of neoliberalism and austerity. It articulates real progress towards a transformed and democratic economy.'

Councillor Matthew Brown, Leader of Preston City Council

T0056398

The Case for Community Wealth Building

The Case For series

Sam Pizzigati, *The Case for a Maximum Wage*

Louise Haagh, *The Case for Universal Basic Income*

James K. Boyce, *The Case for Carbon Dividends*

Frances Coppola, *The Case for People's Quantitative Easing*

Joe Guinan & Martin O'Neill, *The Case for Community Wealth Building*

Joe Guinan

Martin O'Neill

———

The Case for Community Wealth Building

polity

First published in 2020 by Polity Press
Reprinted 2019, 2021, 2022

Polity Press
65 Bridge Street
Cambridge CB2 1UR, UK

Polity Press
101 Station Landing
Suite 300
Medford, MA 02155, USA

ISBN-13: 978-1-5095-3902-4
ISBN-13: 978-1-5095-3903-1(pb)

A catalogue record for this book is available from the British Library.

Typeset in 11 on 15 Sabon by Servis Filmsetting Ltd, Stockport, Cheshire
Printed and bound in Great Britain by CPI Group (UK) Ltd, Croydon

For further information on Polity, visit our website: politybooks.com

For Patricia Harvey and Elizabeth O'Neill

Contents

Preface and Acknowledgements   viii

Introduction: Economic Change, Starting
at the Local Level   1
1   What is Community Wealth Building?   5
2   Taking Control: Arguing for Community
    Wealth Building   36
3   Community Wealth Building and the
    Institutional Turn: Routes to a Democratic
    Economy   81

Further Reading and Resources for Action   117
Notes   118
Index   130

Preface and Acknowledgements

All politics is local.

Tip O'Neill

People live in particular places and in particular communities, and the politics and economics of those places and communities matter hugely for the quality of their lives. These are basic, inescapable facts of human existence, but facts that are often peculiarly overlooked in discussions of social justice and economic policy. And so this is a book about public policy and the pursuit of social justice – but a book whose focus is very much on the local level.

When national governments are pursuing destructive economic policies, action at the local level can be an essential form of protection. More than that, though, and as we argue in this book, local economic policy can be a way of creating plans and models that prefigure large-scale alternatives. The local can be *both* a site of resistance *and* a laboratory for the future, often fulfilling both roles at once.

This book is about the radical potential of 'local justice'. It is written at a time of rapid political and economic flux, when the future paths of our societies are far from certain. Its focus is necessarily on the United States and United Kingdom, the two political economies we know best and where Community Wealth Building is at its most developed – not coincidentally, also the two advanced industrial economies in which neoliberalism was first unleashed, and where its rot runs deepest. We are well aware that there are important, relevant developments in a host of other countries. But personal experience and the need to set some manageable boundaries on the scope of such a short work suggested a narrow focus on Britain and America.

Even a little book like this incurs huge debts of gratitude. Certainly, our various associations with The Democracy Collaborative – the 'think-do tank' based in Washington, DC and Cleveland, Ohio that has been at the forefront of the Community Wealth Building movement in the United States and internationally for two decades – have been formative in our thinking about the development of radical economic alternatives. Joe has been on the staff since 2012, currently serving as Vice President, having previously worked with the Collaborative's principals for four years at its inception back in the early 2000s. Meanwhile Martin has become very much a friend of the TDC family. We are deeply grateful to the executives, staff (past and present), trustees, fellows, and funders of The Democracy Collaborative for their visionary work and leadership.

Gar Alperovitz is a national treasure – if it is permissible to say such a thing of one who has for so long been engaged in opposing American imperium. His decades-long work for transformative social justice and economic system change has bequeathed an intellectual and political legacy that we are only just beginning to get to grips with, now that a new left political movement is emerging. We salute Gar, and remain confident that his greatest contributions lie just around the corner. Ted Howard is an extraordinary social entrepreneur and leader who helped bring the Cleveland Model into being through sheer persistence and force of will. He is a mentor and friend, and it's a privilege to work alongside him. Marjorie Kelly is possessed of a rapier-sharp intellect and a lifelong journalistic commitment to pursuit of the true meaning of things. Her new book with Ted, *The Making of a Democratic Economy*, is a major influence on our thinking. Matthew Brown, principal architect of the Preston Model, is an inspiration; we continue to wish all power to his arm.

At Polity Press, we're grateful to George Owers for his enthusiastic reaction to the idea for this book, and for his efficiency and good judgement. Polity's Julia Davies ably assisted in shepherding the book into existence. We're also grateful to four anonymous referees for their helpful comments on a first draft of the manuscript. All remaining errors are ours alone.

We are also thankful to the many colleagues, friends, and comrades with whom we have been discussing ideas about Community Wealth Building – and the broader agenda for left political economy – during the period in which this book was conceived and written. Thanks in particular to Christine Berry, Juliana Bidadanure, Joe Bilsborough, Grace Blakeley, Fran Boait, Bob Borosage, Miriam Brett, Dana Brown, Adrian Bua, Matthew Butcher, Nick Campbell, Aditya Chakrabortty, Simon Clarke, Michaela Collord, Chiara Cordelli, Andy Cumbers, George Davies, Jonathan Davies, Jurgen De Wispelaere, James Doran, Leah Downey, Steve Dubb, John Duda,

Preface and Acknowledgements

Ander Etxeberria, Laura Flanders, Novak Gajić, Ronnie Galvin, Pablo Gilabert, Peter Gowan, Betty Grdina, Max Harris, Angus Hebenton, Allan Henderson, James Hickson, Dan Hind, Louis-Philippe Hodgson, Cat Hobbs, Jacqui Howard, Diane Ives, Michael Jacobs, Zitto Kabwe, Satoko Kishimoto, Rachel Laurence, Mathew Lawrence, Laurie Laybourn-Langton, Laurie Macfarlane, Neil McInroy, Rory Macqueen, Emily McTernan, James Meadway, Marco Meyer, Keir Milburn, Ed Miliband, Tom Mills, Frances Northrop, Hettie O'Brien, Shin Osawa, Anthony Painter, Simon Parker, Djordje Pavićević, Jules Peck, Kate Pickett, Annie Quick, Luke Raikes, Adam Ramsay, Howard Reed, Duncan Robinson, Miriam Ronzoni, Jessica Rose, Bertie Russell, Kranti Saran, Christian Schemmel, Fabian Schuppert, Asima Shaikh, Hazel Sheffield, Marko Simendić, Clifford Singer, Carla Skandier, Tom Slater, Andrew Small, Kristin Lipke Sparding, Peter Sparding, Gus Speth, James Stafford, Lucas Stanczyk, Amy Studdart, Florence Sutcliffe-Braithwaite, Alan Thomas, Katherine Trebeck, Jens van 't Klooster, Dan Vockins, Hilary Wainwright, Stuart White, Richard Wilkinson, Callum Williams, Madeleine Williams, Thad Williamson, Archie Woodrow, Lea Ypi, and Dave Zuckerman.

We've both had the honour of serving as members of the UK Labour Party's Community Wealth Building Unit, and we are grateful to our colleagues at the unit for stimulating and comradely discussions. Thanks in particular to Mary Robertson and Maryam Eslamdoust of the office of the Leader of the Opposition for creating such a constructive venue for thinking through the potential of Community Wealth Building.

Carys Roberts kindly invited us to publish a preliminary version of parts of Chapter 2 in *IPPR Progressive Review*, and offered helpful comments on earlier versions. Martin is grateful to audiences at the University of Cape Town and the University of York, who gave helpful feedback to talks on 'philosophical foundations for Community Wealth Building'.

The far-sighted funders of The Democracy Collaborative have made many things possible, and Joe is particularly grateful to the Kendeda Fund and NoVo Foundation for their generous longstanding commitments. For financial support, Martin is grateful to the Independent Social Research Foundation (ISRF), a wonderfully agile and imaginative research funder. A Mid-Career Fellowship during the 2017–18 academic year gave valuable space for thinking about issues of power, voice, and economic democracy. From the ISRF, Louise

Braddock, Rachael Kiddey, and Stuart Wilson have been wonderfully wise and supportive. Thanks also to the ISRF and the University of York for jointly funding a stimulating conference on 'Equality and Democracy in Local and City Government' in York in January 2019. Parts of this book were written in the delightful Art Nouveau surroundings of the Writers' House Residence in Tblisi. Martin is grateful to that fascinating institution for its century-old mission of providing a great venue to get some writing done.

We want to give special thanks to two comrades in arms with whom we've worked particularly closely. As Research Director at The Democracy Collaborative, Thomas Hanna has an encyclopaedic knowledge of the democratic economy, and is a brother in the struggle for a postcapitalist world. As Director of European Programs at The Democracy Collaborative, Sarah McKinley has taken the UK work in hand adeptly in her inimitable style, all the while insisting that we have fun – and that the only revolution worth being part of is one in which there is dancing. We're glad to be counted among 'McKinley's Fusiliers'!

Last but not least, we'd like to thank our families. Martin thanks Mary Leng and Tommy, Joe, Olwen, and Rory O'Neill for being the best gang of which one could possibly be a member, and for their patience, love, and sense of fun. Joe sends love to his sister, Lisa North, whose work on the frontlines of our failing system gives her an appreciation of the need for community, and to Roux Robichaux, Peter Harvey, Barbara Harvey, Spencer Rhodes, James Rhodes, Marcia North, and Shane North. He thinks every day of his late father, Martin Guinan, and his unconquerable mind in the service of socialism and peace. And he thanks Emily Robichaux for her support along the way.

Finally, this book is dedicated with much love to our mothers, Pat Harvey and Liz O'Neill, two tough-minded, practical, egalitarian women, from whom we've learned more than we can say.

Introduction: Economic Change, Starting at the Local Level

A new model of economic development is emerging in our cities and communities. Offering real, on-the-ground solutions to localities and regions battered by successive waves of disinvestment, deindustrialisation, displacement, and disempowerment, it is based on a new configuration of economic institutions and approaches capable of producing more sustainable, lasting, and equitable economic outcomes. Rooted in place-based economics, with democratic participation and control, and mobilising the largely untapped power of the local public sector, this emerging approach is also striking for being a transatlantic agenda, one that can find – and is increasingly finding – powerful application in both the United States and United Kingdom. This approach has been termed 'Community Wealth Building'.

The Case for Community Wealth Building

Community Wealth Building is a local economic development strategy focused on building collaborative, inclusive, sustainable, and democratically controlled local economies. Instead of traditional economic development through locational tax incentives, outsourcing, and public-private partnerships, which wastes billions to subsidise the extraction of profit, often by footloose multinational corporations with no loyalty to local communities, Community Wealth Building supports democratic collective ownership of the local economy through a range of institutions and policies. These include worker cooperatives, community land trusts, community development financial institutions, so-called 'anchor institution' procurement strategies, municipal and local public enterprises, and public and community banking.

Based upon the centrality of alternative models of ownership, Community Wealth Building offers the local building blocks by which we can set about a transformation of our economy. Instead of the ongoing concentration of wealth in the hands of a narrow elite, Community Wealth Building pursues a broad dispersal of the ownership of assets. Instead of icily indifferent global markets, it develops the rooted participatory democratic local economy. Instead of the extractive multinational corporation, it is recirculatory, mobilising large place-based economic institutions – such as local government, hospitals, and educational institutions – in support of socially oriented firms that are often democratically owned and controlled by their workers or the community. Instead of outsourcing and asset-stripping privatisation, it turns to plural forms of democratised collective enterprise. Instead of austerity and private credit creation by *rentier* finance, Community Wealth Building looks to the huge potential power of community and state banks and public money creation. And on and on. Viewed in this way, Community Wealth Building is economic system change, but starting at the local level.

In this short book, we explore the history and rapidly emerging potential of this radical approach to local economic development. Chapter 1 explains the central features of Community Wealth Building as a strategy for economic development, and charts the recent history of this approach. Chapter 2 looks at the justification for this kind of strategy, grounding a case for Community Wealth Building in values of social justice, equality, and democracy, while also responding to some important lines of criticism. Chapter 3 concludes by considering Community Wealth Building in the context of what we call the 'institutional turn' in radical approaches to political economy, examining its potential as part of a broader overall strategy for forging a new political-economic system capable of responding to the large-order threats of the day, from ecological breakdown to the perilous rise of the neo-populist far right.

As is inevitably the case with such a brief work, we offer what follows as a starting point for these important discussions rather than any kind of claim to definitiveness. This book is certainly not the last word on Community Wealth Building, but we do hope that it will be a helpful stimulus to further debate and discussion on this exciting, radical, and rapidly advancing agenda.

1

What Is Community Wealth Building?

In this opening chapter we review the origins of the emerging movement for Community Wealth Building in the overlapping crises facing our communities, and the rising levels of social and economic pain that are compelling more and more people to take action themselves locally on the basis of resources and strategies that are readily at hand, even in some of our poorest communities and regions. We offer a working definition drawn from the leading organisations pursuing these strategies, highlighting the main principles of Community Wealth Building as it is being put into practice, and briefly survey the current state of the field, with attention to two flagship initiatives on either side of the Atlantic – the Cleveland and Preston Models.

Community Wealth Building is based upon

economic interventions that seek to intervene not 'after the fact', in an attempt to redistribute the economic gains from a lopsided economic model, but by reconfiguring the core institutional relationships of the economy in order to produce better, more egalitarian outcomes as part of its routine operations and normal functioning. As such, it represents in microcosm a new approach to a more democratic economy. Such an approach offers a wider promise, not just delivering for local communities but also helping us all, as democratic citizens, to imagine, experience, and get involved with systemic economic transformation. Communities that are experimenting with Community Wealth Building strategies can thus be seen as 'laboratories of democracy', pointing the way towards future economic models that can have a broader range of application in recasting the terms of our political and economic life at the scale of the nation as a whole – and perhaps even beyond.

The rise of Community Wealth Building institutions, as a matter of practical experimentation in real places by ordinary people, shows that alternatives capable of moving us away from neoliberal austerity in the direction of democratised ownership of the economy do in fact exist. They are already being put into practice around the world, and are ripe for wider deployment. They provide a way to connect with the grassroots energy and organising potential of existing social movements and a newly emerging political radicalism reluctant to engage with the discredited business-as-usual official politics of recent decades. On both sides of the Atlantic, Community Wealth Building presents a potential basis for a new institutional underpinning for egalitarian politics, building local support for new economic models and approaches from the ground up in a way that is less daunting and more comprehensible than it can sometimes appear at the national level.

In their recent book, *The Making of a Democratic Economy*, Marjorie Kelly and Ted Howard of The Democracy Collaborative, two of the leading thinkers and practitioners of Community Wealth Building, argue that it is possible to detect in scattered experiments across the United States and around the world something that 'many of us hunger for but can scarcely imagine is possible ... an economy of, by, and for the people'. They go on to delineate the principles of an emerging 'coherent paradigm for how to organise an economy' that point to a possible next system beyond the current crisis-ridden neoliberal economic model:

> The first moral principles of this system are community and sustainability, for as indigenous peoples have long known, the two are one and the same. Other principles are creating opportunities for those long excluded, and putting labor before capital; ensuring that assets are broadly held, and that investing is for people and place, with profit the result, not the primary aim; designing enterprises for a new era of equity and sustainability; and evolving ownership beyond a primitive notion of maximum extraction to an advanced concept of stewardship.[1]

This emerging *democratic economy* stands in stark contrast to the existing *extractive economy* that is designed to generate maximum financial returns and distribute them upwards to the tiny elite that currently owns and controls the lion's share of productive assets. Far from being unattainable pie in the sky, this vision of a democratic economy and the principles that underpin it have been distilled from painstaking observation of the pattern of popular experimentation in a host of communities across the globe – the result of an explosion of local innovation in response to the ravages of decades of neoliberal extraction.

It is a central part of the argument of this book that the case for Community Wealth Building should be made through seeing such policies and approaches as part of the broader movement to create more democratic economies, and to move us beyond the depredations of the failed neoliberal experiment. But before taking up this broader agenda, we will first focus on the recent history of Community Wealth Building. In some central respects, it is a tale of two cities: Cleveland, Ohio; and Preston, Lancashire. It is to those two cities that we will now turn.

Two Models of Community Wealth Building: Cleveland and Preston

Community Wealth Building represents an alternative to the conventional economic development model. The term first emerged in the United States in 2005, and was coined by The Democracy Collaborative. The ideas behind Community Wealth Building are not new, although in some cases they have taken novel forms. In fact, they hearken back to longstanding traditions on the left of libertarian socialism and economic democracy. As Steve Dubb, Ted Howard, and Sarah McKinley have summarised it, the core idea of *economic democracy* involves extending democratic principles of popular sovereignty from the realm of governance and politics to the operations and institutions of the economy itself – and Community Wealth Building is one of the frameworks within which economic democracy is increasingly being applied:

> *Community wealth building* emphasizes the importance of placing control of wealth in the hands of locally rooted forms of business enterprise, with ownership vested in community stakeholders, through a range of forms including cooperative, employee, public, or nonprofit ownership. Community ownership makes it possible to reinvest profits locally and thus reduces the financial leakage out of communities. Economically, it allows local publics to exert democratic control over local government; policy-wise, it allows them to achieve sustainability and equitable development goals.[2]

There are now two flagship models of Community Wealth Building – and a growing number of additional emerging experiments and innovations in cities across the United States and United Kingdom.

The original model of Community Wealth Building is the Evergreen Cooperatives in Cleveland, Ohio. Cleveland lost half its population and most of its Fortune 500 companies due to deindustrialisation, disinvestment, and capital flight. But it still had very large nonprofit and quasi-public institutions such as the Cleveland Clinic, Case Western Reserve University, and University Hospitals – known as *anchor institutions* because they are rooted in place and aren't likely to up and leave. Together these three institutions, themselves largely dependent on flows of public funds and favourable tax treatment, spent around $3 billion per year – very little of which was going to the local community.

The Democracy Collaborative worked with the anchors, the city, and the Cleveland Foundation to pursue a strategy to localise their procurement in support of a network of purposely created green worker co-ops – the Evergreen Cooperatives – tied together in a community corporation. These include an industrial-scale ecologically advanced laundry, a large urban greenhouse, and a renewable energy company. A fund has recently been added to pursue employee ownership conversions of existing businesses. Linked by a community-serving nonprofit corporation and a revolving fund, the Evergreen companies cannot easily be sold outside the network, and return a percentage of their profits to develop additional worker-owned firms and grow the local economy. Unlike conventional corporations, these democratic businesses will not pick up and move their jobs to another location. Through such strategies – the opposite of

11

neoliberal extraction – money can be kept circulating, anchoring jobs and building community wealth, reversing long-term economic decline. Today the Evergreen companies are profitable and competing with the multinational corporations that had previously provided contract services to the big anchor institutions.

Meanwhile, Community Wealth Building approaches have crossed the Atlantic to the United Kingdom, where they are being taken up and developed with ever-growing sophistication and impact. Back in 2012 the example of Cleveland caught the attention of a young Labour councillor, Matthew Brown – now the Leader of Preston City Council. With the collapse of a plan for major private sector investment – the ill-fated Tithebarn project – Preston had been left high and dry by its conventional economic development approach. With the help of others such as Neil McInroy of the Manchester-based Centre for Local Economic Strategies (CLES), Brown took up the Cleveland Model and radically expanded it. The Preston Model, as it has become known, encompasses a string of public sector anchors across Preston and Lancashire, to which Brown and his colleagues have added public pension investment and affordable housing, while laying the groundwork for the development of a community bank. Carried out in the teeth of austerity and cuts to local government budgets, Preston's work in Community Wealth Building has received favourable attention across the UK media, being profiled by *The Economist*, *Guardian*, BBC News, *Mirror*, and *Sunday Times*, amongst other outlets.

Once a poster child for economic deprivation and 'left behind' places, Preston has already seen significant payoffs from its alternative economic development approach, having been named the UK's most improved urban area. As George Eaton wrote in the *New Statesman*:

> the share of the public procurement budget spent in the city has risen from 5 per cent in 2013 to 18 per cent (a gain of £75m), while across Lancashire it has risen from 39 per cent to 79 per cent (a gain of £200m). Unemployment has fallen from 6.5 per cent in 2014 to 3.1 per cent and ... Preston has also achieved above-average improvements for health, transport, work-life balance, and youth and adult skills.[3]

A new radical agenda for local government is clearly emerging, and a great deal of energy is being generated by the prospect of turning this activist, democratic, and egalitarian model of local government into a new consensus about how local democratic institutions should operate. It is striking that this new vision is taking hold on both sides of the Atlantic, with cities and localities in both Britain and the United States finding ways to short-circuit and move beyond the previously entrenched technocratic local government approach. When even the professional services firm PricewaterhouseCoopers, in their annual report on *Good Growth for Cities*, lauds the City of Preston as the UK's most improved place to live, then it is clear that the ground is starting to shift in mainstream understandings of the role and scope of local authorities in shaping their local economies.[4] What might once have seemed like a fringe idea is moving fast towards supplanting the old mainstream approach, entrenching a new way of thinking about how local government should act, and how ambitious politicians can be in looking to shape their local economies in a more egalitarian direction.

These promising alternatives are now being taken up and applied far and wide – in America from New York City to Albuquerque, New Mexico, and from Miami, Florida to Richmond, Virginia, and in Britain from Hackney and Islington to Manchester and Hartlepool. There is considerable interest in such approaches from a rising new generation of progressive political leaders. In the meantime, a head of steam is building at the national level. Embracing the billing of Preston as 'Jeremy Corbyn's Model Town', a Community Wealth Building Unit has been set up in the Labour leader's office. This unit promotes these kinds of common-sense practical local strategies for democratising the economy among councillors and local authorities, and aims to provide technical assistance and capacity building. There is also growing interest in the approach on other parts of the political spectrum, including in the Scottish National Party and even from the UK Cabinet Office.

Looking ahead, it's possible to imagine such approaches taken to a national scale. The UK's National Health Service (NHS) has already embraced the anchor mission as part of its long-term plan. With its massive purchasing power and economic footprint, the NHS could serve as the mother of all anchor institutions, the backbone of a series of regional industrial strategies by which health-related goods and services would be provided as part of ensuring the health and well-being of communities. Thus the new economic paradigm starts to achieve scale and take powerful shape before our eyes.

Community Wealth Building represents in microcosm a new approach to a more democratic economy. The manner in which Preston has evidently caught the imagination as a proving ground for the new economics points to the wider role such strategies can play, not just in delivering for their local communities but also in helping us all to imagine, experience, and get involved with systemic economic transformation. As we argue further in Chapters 2 and 3, communities that are experimenting with strategies of Community Wealth Building can be seen as 'laboratories of democracy', pointing the way towards future economic models that can have a broader range of application.

There is abundant evidence that the existing neoliberal economic model is failing most people. But often what holds a system in place is a failure to imagine that things can fundamentally change, that there are real, viable alternatives for organising a different system. There is an urgent need for an inspiring politics of reconstruction, one capable of balancing realism about current possibilities with an insistence upon retaining a political-economic project aimed at a future beyond the cramped and impoverished horizons of the present. Part of the answer lies in on-the-ground experimentation and model-building that embraces the design and principles of a new alternative capable of producing vastly improved economic, social, and ecological outcomes as a matter of course.

Origins of Community Wealth Building: A Response to Crisis and Pain

The context in which Community Wealth Building models are emerging is one of long-running social and economic crisis. Among the first to succumb to what became four decades of neoliberal economic policies, the United States and United Kingdom are facing profound systemic crises, not merely political or economic difficulties. For the majority, the economy is in stagnation. Many communities are in decay. The lives of millions are compromised by economic and social pain. A generation of young people now expects to be worse off than their parents. Climate change represents an existential threat to our ability to maintain an organised global community.

Across a range of socio-economic indicators, the data make for grim reading. To take the United States as only the most extreme example, real wages for roughly 80 per cent of American workers have been virtually flat for at least three decades. It's hard to convey the full magnitude of the economic destruction visited upon America's manufacturing heartland. In a great arc running from upstate New York, Pennsylvania, and Ohio into Indiana, Illinois, Michigan, and Wisconsin, community after community has been destabilised by successive waves of deindustrialisation. Whole cities have been thrown away, entire regions left behind, as firms picked up and moved elsewhere – first to the non-union Sunbelt, then to Mexico and China – leaving behind empty factories and houses, and half-empty schools and hospitals. The capital, carbon, and human costs have been immense. Cleveland has lost half a million people since 1950, 57 per cent of its population. In Detroit, it's more than a million, over 60 per cent; of those remaining, over a third live below the poverty line.

The seeds of destruction were sown in the corporate restructurings of the 1970s and 1980s, which saw massive downsizings and layoffs on behalf of an aggressive pursuit of shareholder value. Workers' own savings were mobilised against them, the huge pools of capital accumulated by their occupational pension funds used by the financial services industry to export their jobs through overseas investment. Then came the ramming through, in the Clinton era, of the remainder of the neoliberal programme. Repeated rounds of trade liberalisation have caused the United States to run a goods trade deficit every year since 1976. Over 5 million manufacturing jobs have been lost since the North American Free Trade Agreement (NAFTA) came into effect, the bulk of them since 2000 and the establishment of permanent normal trade relations (PNTR) with China.

For the American worker, these were locust years – decades of low growth, high unemployment, and rising inequality. Virtually all the economic gains have been captured by the very rich. Inequality has reached Gilded Age levels, with the top 1 per cent now claiming 22 per cent of all income – their largest share since 1929. Wealth is even more concentrated, with the top 10 per cent commanding three quarters of the total, while the bottom 60 per cent have seen their wealth fall. Forty per cent of families are living from payday to payday, with almost no savings to fall back on in the event of job loss, sickness, or other emergency. The Obama economy saw the weakest, most lopsided recovery from any of the eleven recessions since 1945.

Anger is already boiling over at a system people know is stacked against them. A Reuters/Ipsos poll on the day of the 2016 US presidential election found 72 per cent agreeing that 'the economy is rigged to advantage the rich and powerful'.[5] Donald Trump ran hard against neoliberal finance and trade in both the primaries and the 2016 general election. There's no doubt that many blue-collar voters in the abandoned towns of the rustbelt and rural Appalachia were willing to give him a chance.

Trump flipped a third of counties previously carried by Obama twice. With them came the electoral votes of Pennsylvania, Ohio, Michigan, Wisconsin, and Iowa – and the White House.

The United Kingdom, while it hasn't quite reached these levels of difficulty, is not far behind. The UK now boasts the greatest regional economic disparities in Europe. While central London is the richest region in Europe, the UK nevertheless has six of the ten poorest regions in Northern Europe, with West Wales, Cornwall, Lincolnshire, South Yorkshire, and the Tees Valley being listed by Eurostat, the EU's statistical agency, as the five poorest regions across ten countries in Northern and Western Europe. While the income share of the top 1 per cent in the UK has almost trebled since the start of the 'neoliberal period', rising from under 6 per cent of total income in 1979 to almost 15 per cent in 2013, British workers have been facing the longest squeeze on their wages since the Napoleonic Wars, with average wages still lower (when adjusted for inflation) than they were before the financial crisis of 2007–8, creating a 'lost decade' for British workers unprecedented outside of wartime. (Only with the First and Second World Wars have there been similar periods of real wage stagnation.)[6]

In the face of such challenges, traditional strategies to achieve equitable and sustainable social, economic, and ecological outcomes simply no longer work. Income and wealth disparities have become severe. The government no longer has much capacity to use progressive taxation to achieve equity goals or to regulate corporations effectively. A growing number of people have begun to ask ever more penetrating questions about the direction in which things are headed. When big problems emerge across the entire spectrum of national life, it cannot be for small reasons. A political economy is a system, and today's system is programmed not to meet basic needs but to prioritise the generation of corporate profits, the growth of GDP, and the projection of geopolitical power. Anyone serious about addressing these challenges needs to think through and then build a new political economy, no matter how difficult the task or how long it takes. Systemic problems require systemic solutions.[7]

There is an urgent need to rise to the challenge of this era of pain and difficulty. The need today is to begin advancing a practicable alternative economics commensurate with the enormity of the task of community stabilisation and reconstruction. Hanging in the balance is the tattered fabric of the social safety net and those programmes that represent a last remaining bulwark against the current system's

vastly unequal outcomes. Meanwhile, a new revan-
chist far right is already on the march. Unless an
alternative can be found, we must prepare ourselves for some devastating fiscal, regulatory, and
policy setbacks across the board. There's important
work to be done defending those individuals and
communities most at risk. At the same time, we
simply cannot allow ourselves to be trapped on the
defensive. There is a pressing need to put forward
a positive, community-building plan that combines
resistance with the scaling up of new models and
institutions, all the while developing compelling
analytical frameworks supportive of a new politics
and economics.

Many are turning to their local economies as an
important locus of struggle. The hope is that cities
can serve as laboratories for economic alternatives
and preserve the critical political and policy space in
which to move forward even in advance of national
electoral victory. This will require confronting
the grotesque power that corporations currently
wield over local communities and public authorities through their locational decisions. In truth,
cities need not be so powerless. Their own economic footprint as the local public sector, combined
with associated spending by institutions stewarding
public funds, is sufficiently large that, used more

purposefully, it could stabilise local economies on the basis of sticky capital and anchored jobs. This in turn would reduce corporate leverage and restore the capacity for real democratic local economic decision-making.

The Emerging Mosaic: Elements of the Democratic Economy

Conventional policies and approaches are demonstrably failing to alter deteriorating long-running trends on income inequality, concentrated wealth, community divestment and displacement, persistent place- and race-based poverty, and environmental destruction. As a consequence, recent years have witnessed an upsurge of practical experimentation with a variety of alternative economic institutions and models that are capable of fundamentally altering patterns of ownership and producing dramatically better distributional (and other) outcomes. Taken together, these institutions and approaches form the mosaic of a new democratic economy in the making, suggesting the contours of a next system beyond neoliberalism along with some pathways for getting there.[8]

In community after community on both sides

of the Atlantic this is already beginning to occur. Social pain is intensifying, but something else is happening too. In the United States, in central city neighbourhoods that have long suffered high levels of unemployment and poverty, a new dynamic has been developing. Because public expenditures for jobs and housing have been deemed politically impossible, more and more people are embracing economic alternatives in which new wealth is built from the bottom up, collectively.

The Democracy Collaborative has been surveying the emerging mosaic of this new democratic economy in the United States for two decades. What are these developments? They include social enterprises that undertake businesses to support social missions. They include nonprofit community development corporations (CDCs) – more than 5,000 of them, some dating back to the original radical economic programme of the civil rights movement – together with hundreds of community land trusts (CLTs), both of which develop and maintain low-income housing and seek to prevent gentrification and displacement. They include community development financial institutions (CDFIs), which invest in creating jobs and housing and providing services for poor and underserved communities; from around $4 billion a year a decade ago, community investment has grown in scale and importance to more than $60 billion today. They include a rise in worker ownership – whether in the form of Employee Stock Ownership Plans (ESOPs) or fully-fledged worker cooperatives like Cooperative Home Care Associates (CHCA) in the Bronx, the largest worker co-op in America, made up of some 2,300 predominantly female workers, most of them immigrant women of colour, about half of whom are worker-owners. Some 11,000 businesses in America are now owned in whole or in part by their employees, involving over 10 million workers – 3 million more than are members of trade unions in the private sector.

This is no longer small-scale stuff: 130 million Americans – one in three – are now members of one or another form of urban, agricultural, or financial cooperative. Credit unions – one member one vote democratic banks – collectively serve 90 million Americans while holding around $1 trillion in assets, making them as large, taken together, as one of the biggest Wall Street banks, knocking Goldman Sachs out of the top five.

Then there is the role of 'anchor institutions' – large nonprofit institutions like universities and hospitals ('eds and meds', in the economic development jargon) that tend not to move location.

These institutions have a huge economic footprint. America's colleges and universities collectively hold endowments worth half a trillion dollars. In terms of procurement, hospitals and universities represent over $1 trillion in annual spending. They are frequently located next door to some of the poorest and most disinvested communities. Their operations offer a way to scale up Community Wealth Building strategies.

In the public sector, state and local government economic development programmes invest in local businesses while municipal enterprises build infrastructure and provide services, raising revenue and creating employment, diversifying the base of locally controlled capital. Public utilities, together with co-ops, currently provide a quarter of America's electricity. Across the United States, from California to Alabama, public pension assets are being channelled into job creation and community development. Twenty states, and a growing number of cities, are looking into the creation of public banking systems like North Dakota's, widely credited with ensuring that the state had no bank failures and a lower unemployment rate during the financial crisis and Great Recession – developments that if enacted would allow for democratic authority over, and community benefit from, critical investment decisions. Trusts that allow for public ownership and management of natural resources provide revenue streams from capital, recalling the ideas for collective asset ownership – through forms of 'citizens' trusts' – of the late Nobel Prize-winning economist James Meade.[9]

From parks and blood banks to libraries and the internet, commons management systems can provide an expanding zone of decommodification to buffer against the market. Public trusts can be extended into additional domains, from land to the electromagnetic spectrum, underwriting public services or issuing a citizen dividend. Community control of land can ensure affordable housing and prevent disruptive gentrification and speculative real estate bubbles. All in all, it is becoming possible to project a vision of democratised municipal and regional economies, oriented towards local multipliers – the additional economic benefit generated by keeping money circulating and recirculating locally – as an alternative to neoliberal austerity and extraction.

These institutional developments and innovations involve design principles for rooting capital in place, maximising local multipliers, and preventing the leakages that come with the neoliberal model. It's a vision of democratic local and regional economies in which we take in each other's wake, creating shared value and building assets that are held collectively by small and large publics.[10] They point to a strategy for the *de-globalisation of capital*, and therefore represent a real and concrete response to some of the massive forces that have been driving inequality and destroying communities for decades. Worker-owned firms, cooperatives, anchor institutions, community land trusts, community corporations – none of them are likely to up and relocate offshore.

As we contemplate the loss of a generation to austerity, it is becoming essential to move beyond defensive rearguard actions on ever more unfavourable terrain and to actually go on the offensive. The steadily building array of alternative economic institutions and the Community Wealth Building principles they embody offer ways to do this. As well as building new wealth from the bottom up they offer the prospect of the weakening and displacement of corporate power and finance and their grip on our economies. By extending new institutional experiments and the principles behind them we can begin to sketch the outlines of a new economic framework based on the democratisation of wealth. This offers not merely new hope for a left that has spent decades out in the cold but also points to the possibility of generating a new economic paradigm that could eventually displace neoliberalism.

This can only occur by going beyond failing defensive strategies of after-the-fact intervention and redistribution and moving instead to a new institutional settlement and a new orientation in our thinking about political economy. The accompanying table captures the contrast between the exhausted conventional approach to community economic development and the promise by comparison of new Community Wealth Building strategies.

The prevailing paradigm of community economic development is clearly broken. Under neoliberalism, cities and states are encouraged to compete fiercely with one another for jobs and investment in a context of corporate locational blackmail or extortion. This plays out as a zero-sum – sometimes negative-sum! – game hugely beneficial to corporations but far less so for localities and ordinary people, as could be seen in the egregious race to the bottom on corporate subsidies unleashed by the competition among US cities to attract the new Amazon headquarters.[11] The conventional economic development model often requires upwards of $100,000 in taxpayer-funded inducements *per job created*.[12] And, of course, these supposedly 'new' jobs are

The Case for Community Wealth Building

Two Approaches to Economic Development

Drivers	Conventional Approach	Community Wealth Building
Place	Aims to attract firms using incentives, which increases the tax burden on local residents.	Develops under-utilised local assets of many kinds, for the benefit of local residents.
Ownership	Supports absentee and elite ownership, often harming locally owned family firms.	Promotes local, broad-based ownership as the foundation of a thriving local economy.
Multipliers	Pays scant attention to whether money is leaking out of a community.	Encourages institutional buy-local strategies to keep money circulating locally.
Collaboration	Decision-making led primarily by government and private sector, excluding local residents.	Brings many players to the table: nonprofits, philanthropy, anchors, and cities.
Inclusion	Key metric is number of jobs created, with little regard for wages or who is hired.	Aims to create inclusive, living wage jobs that help all families enjoy economic security.
Workforce	Relies on generalised training programmes without a focus on linkages to actual jobs.	Links training to employment and focuses on jobs for those with barriers to employment.
System	Accepts status quo of wealth inequality, hoping benefits will trickle down.	Develops institutions and supportive ecosystems to create a new normal of broad-based economic activity.

Source: Marjorie Kelly and Sarah McKinley, *Cities Building Community Wealth* (The Democracy Collaborative, 2015).

often not really new jobs at all, but jobs that were formerly elsewhere. When the subsidies expire, the game is often played out all over again, with a new city as victim of the corporate shakedown.

Viewed from the perspective of the economy as a whole, this becomes the 'throw-away cities' phenomenon in which entire cities are discarded at immense capital and carbon (not to mention human!) costs – only for them to have to be built all over again in new locations.[13] As previously noted, Detroit is only among the more extreme examples, having lost more than a million people since 1950. Of those that remain, one in three are below the poverty line – including one in three children who live in households at less than 50 per cent of the poverty line. A similar pattern can be found in any number of America's other rustbelt cities. These long-running trends have their roots in massive global economic forces, including financialisation, deindustrialisation, and the relentless pursuit of maximising shareholder value. Although they pre-date the Great Financial Crisis, that crisis has only made them worse.

The Case for Community Wealth Building

A New Institutional Settlement?

All too often, we do not talk enough about institutions when we talk about politics and policies. Institutions are critically important. The institutional underpinnings of the postwar settlement were strong organised labour movements and mass political parties together with a national Keynesian economic framework. That institutional basis is gone – probably for good. For the left under neoliberalism, the house always wins. The right is in power even when it is out of office, through the banks and all the other sources of institutional power in the economy. The previous social democratic strategy of 'after the fact' intervention to adjust the 'normal' outcomes of the economy is a precarious one in political economy terms because it involves working against the grain of the system. Even when incremental progress is made it is difficult to sustain over time and can easily be reversed. It is past time to get much more ambitious, and to start laying the groundwork for a new set of institutional arrangements that in and of themselves produce improved outcomes through the normal functioning of the economy. Community Wealth Building offers a way to begin doing this at the local level, on the basis of resources and institutions that are already available and ready to hand.

The postwar consensus is now but a distant memory, while more recent strategies of accommodation to neoliberalism in order to skim the surplus for ameliorative social spending have collapsed with the end of the 'long bubble' upon which they depended. A grim new era of economic difficulty stretches ahead, one likely to be characterised by sluggish growth punctuated by stagnation. All but inevitably on the present course, powerful underlying trends will continue to drive outcomes, as yawning inequality, underemployment, poverty, and ecological despoliation deepen day by day.

Addressing the growing problems of the twenty-first century requires going beyond business-as-usual to embrace a radically different pattern of political economy capable of delivering fundamental social and economic change. At the heart of today's capitalism is a set of institutional relationships – private credit creation, capital markets, giant publicly traded corporations – that together form the most powerful engine for the extraction of value the world has ever seen. 'Its purpose', as Marjorie Kelly insists, 'is manufacturing financial wealth in endlessly growing quantity.'[14] It is this set of relationships, this basic institutional design, that drives the outcomes we are seeing in terms of labour arbitrage, compounding inequality, social atomisation, and environmental destruction.

For a time, it proved possible to offset such outcomes using regulation and redistribution. But the institutional underpinnings of the postwar consensus – strong organised labour movements, mass political parties, an economic framework based on demand management – are long gone. Patterns evident in the previous, Victorian era of globalisation have resumed. With financialisation, offshoring, and corporate restructuring, the capacity of governments around the world to hold the line against rising inequality – *even when they actually wish to do so* – is ever more reduced. If the underlying trends are to be altered it is no longer possible to sidestep fundamental questions of ownership and control. Ultimately, a truly impactful alternative strategy must go after capital itself.

Twice since the Second World War radical political shifts have brought about transformations of the economies of the United Kingdom and the United States by changing the underlying institutions and ownership patterns – first Keynesianism, then neoliberalism. Each in their own way set the terms for the decades that followed. With the increasingly evident exhaustion of the neoliberal model, the search is on for the next political-economic paradigm capable of replacing it. Community Wealth Building is a way to start at the local level and begin creating systemic economic change that can, in the end, bring about a fundamental shift in the balance of power and wealth in favour of ordinary people.

We are once again in a time of great flux and change. Left strategy needs to rise to the occasion. Having been dealt out of the game for so long, suddenly there is everything to play for again. As popular movements and new institutional developments converge, there is the glimpse of a new world in the making. Community Wealth Building is one of the pathways by which we can get there.

2

Taking Control: Arguing for Community Wealth Building

This chapter moves from the 'what' of Community Wealth Building to the 'why'. We set out the justification for the strategy of Community Wealth Building, grounding the case in values of social justice, equality, and democracy, while also responding to some important lines of criticism that such approaches may face.

Justifying Community Wealth Building

The first step in justifying the adoption of Community Wealth Building is realising the importance of taking our values seriously. In order to have the hope of achieving a transformation in how the economy can be made to serve people's real interests, we need to be able to make demands for economic change that are clear and explicit about what we want economic institutions to do for us. If we value social justice, economic control, democracy, and social equality, then we need to embed those values into our democratic and economic institutions. One of the most dangerous and corrosive aspects of the neoliberal era has been the way in which an emphasis on the economic bottom line has been pushed so far that we can lose confidence in advancing arguments and justifications in the public realm that depend on values other than economic efficiency.[1] But this failure of confidence is as unnecessary as it is politically disastrous. While there is often a strong case even in narrowly economic terms for the pursuit of Community Wealth Building strategies, we should not be reluctant, when supporting radical local economic strategies, to appeal to our central political values of equality, democracy, and social justice.

We should want to have political and economic institutions that are justifiable to those who fall under their influence, and whose lives are lived in part in the social and economic landscape that those institutions help create. Our aim should therefore be to create an economy that serves the real needs and interests of our fellow citizens. When we think about the structure and development of our economic and political institutions, we need to consider both narrowly economic and more broadly evaluative considerations. We need the courage of our convictions, and a readiness to push ahead with a more human way of thinking and talking about the economy, and about economic policy, that acknowledges that the economy is a realm in which our values are in danger of being betrayed when they are not actively advanced.

We have written elsewhere about the idea of an 'institutional turn' in progressive thinking about the economy – the idea that a more egalitarian and democratic society cannot be achieved through piecemeal redistribution within the outdated and inadequate economic institutions that we already have, but will require an ambitious reimagining of the institutional architecture of the economy.[2] Community Wealth Building is one especially powerful and fertile element within that broader institutional project.

We start below by making the positive normative case for Community Wealth Building, and by relating these economic strategies to values of justice, equality, and democracy. We then move on to countering the most common and powerful lines of objection to these kinds of local economic strategies, considering some lines of objection pursued by critics of the approach. Although much of what one reads in the way of critique of Community Wealth Building is misdirected or implausible, there are nevertheless some important challenges to these approaches which are often made in good faith, and which merit careful engagement and rebuttal. We hope that the latter sections of this chapter manage that task of countering the critics of Community Wealth Building. But first we start with the positive case.

Political Values and Public Control

The range of values that are at stake in assessing public policy go well beyond the personal or commercial values that would typically be associated with economic transactions within the market. But the place of political values in local government – values such as equality, democracy, and social cohesion – has been eroded in recent years, during a period where there has been both extensive outsourcing of public services, and often also a parallel narrowing in mindset within the public sector. One effect of the neoliberal orientation of the doctrines of 'New Public Management' is that even those working within the public sector have increasingly taken on an outlook more closely aligned to private sector commercial enterprises, where narrow issues of economic cost are taken to be central in understandings of value. As practitioners at the Centre for Local Economic Strategies have argued, the public sector has increasingly become overly focused on the cost of everything, losing track of the real value of its activities, which should run well beyond anything that could be captured within a purely economic metric.[3]

Nevertheless, in the United Kingdom the groundwork for the reversal of this process, and for the rediscovery of a broader set of political values in public policy, has already been put in place with the enactment of the 2012 Social Value Act. This legislation has opened the way for public institutions such as local authorities to look beyond a solely economistic conception of their work, and instead think in a broader way about the normative underpinnings of what they are trying to achieve, expanding a narrow focus on cost with a broader concern with social outcomes. The impact of this legislation has so far been minimal, with the terms of the Act often requiring only what amounts to a scant or superficial assessment of non-economic considerations when public institutions grant contracts or procure goods and services, in many cases no more than a kind of perfunctory 'tick-box' exercise in which private contractors are simply invited to make a few symbolic genuflections towards the idea of 'corporate social responsibility'.[4] The direction of travel is the right one, but the speed of movement towards re-embracing ideas of public and social value is as yet inadequate.

We need a more radical change, thinking in a much more imaginative and ambitious way about how public institutions function at every level, emphasising that local government and local public institutions are not merely market participants in commercial exchanges, but rather institutions that help to create the economic and political landscape in which citizens live their lives. Consider the case of a local authority purchasing social care provision. It could see its role here as no more than that of a quasi-commercial intermediary, looking to purchase a certain suite of human services at a best cost price, thereby delivering best value to local taxpayers. Or it could view itself as something different, as part of the underlying structure of a locality and a local community. It could view itself as a public institution that relates to local people in a variety of ways and guises, as both an employer as well as a service provider. And it could see its central mission as not only to deliver certain services at an efficient cost with the resources at its disposal, but also more broadly as helping to construct the social and economic landscape in which people live.

Once we see public institutions for what they really are, or what they really can be – as institutions that have an anchoring role in grounding the norms and expectations of a society, and not just as one kind of participant in market exchanges – then there is compelling reason to accept this expansion of the range of relevant values appropriate to their assessment and evaluation. It would not be enough, to take this one example, to provide social care at the lowest possible cost, if that means buying a service that involves exploitative employment practices, with workers treated merely as a cheap resource to be deployed for maximum 'output' at minimum cost – as, for example, Gateshead in the North East of England has done, in employing casual labour on zero-hour contracts. Individual workers are also members of the community, entitled to being treated with respect, and to terms of employment that give them dignity and security. Individual service providers are not merely a cost to be minimised, but, just like those to whom they provide services, members of the broader community.

The ambition of a local authority in procuring

social care services, then, should not just be the low-cost provision of a kind of fictitious commodity to those who need it, but instead the creation of a public institution in which both those receiving the services and those providing them are treated with care and respect, and where that public institution has a crucial role in creating the conditions in which mutual relations of care, recognition, and respect can develop and flourish. Of course, this is not an easy goal to achieve, and austerity policies and slashed budgets can make achieving it much harder. But this is the kind of ambition that local authorities should have, and there is a real loss when inadequate budgets make its realisation impossible.

Given the role of local authorities in shaping the social landscape, and their *ineradicably public* nature, it is always a kind of moral error, even a kind of category mistake, to take an excessively narrow, cost-based approach to thinking about spending by public institutions, which is after all done both for our benefit and that of our fellow citizens, and also in our name. In short, when we think seriously about the justification of economic policy, at the local as much as at the national level, our way of thinking must not be one that sets values aside, misconceiving the public domain as merely an arena of cost-driven transactions. Instead, it should be a way of thinking that is true to our values, and unafraid to give them expression.

The substantive focus of our argument is on how a way of thinking about what we might call 'local justice' should be seen in terms of the ambition of creating more egalitarian and more democratic local communities. One way of thinking about this is in terms of democratic control of the economy. When local public institutions adopt a narrow 'best-cost' approach that sees everything only in terms of prices within an already existing market, there is a loss of any sense of public control over the longer-run trajectory of a community. Instead, we are simply left buffeted by economic forces beyond our control. A shift to a more activist outlook regarding public institutions, including an acknowledgement of their role in shaping the economy rather than just participating in it, brings with it a change in outlook from the reactive to the active, a shift from lacking control to taking control over our collective destinies.

When Preston City Council Leader Matthew Brown, the pioneer of the Preston Model, talks about the goals of Community Wealth Building, the idea of control is at the centre of his vision. As he puts it:

> You can create alternatives within local communities, where the predominant way of doing things is one in which the community takes control of its own destiny through capturing the wealth and putting it under democratic control ... if you go to Bologna in Italy, if you go to Mondragón in the Basque Country, the wage level is about twenty per cent or thirty per cent higher than in the rest of the country because they've found a way of capturing wealth and putting it in the hands of the people who produce it, the workers, instead of outside company owners who often come and go at a whim, taking that surplus out of the area.[5]

We might therefore take the view that this kind of 'taking control' is good insofar as it allows a reallocation of returns from capital to labour; hence, it can be seen as a necessary precondition for generating more equal economic outcomes. But we may also take the view that this kind of taking control is *also* valuable in a more direct, non-instrumental way. There is a value to a community using its collective institutions to take charge of its collective destiny, exerting itself politically, and turning those institutions into a democratic instrument for pursuing collective values, rather than letting them atrophy. Taking democratic control over the local economic landscape is, then, both intrinsically a way of turning our commitment to democracy into something real in the world, and at the same time a means towards reducing socioeconomic inequality through a more activist model of local government.

In the following three sections, we will elaborate on this idea of taking control of local economies, developing it in terms of the values of democracy and equality, before going on to show how those two values are deeply interrelated.

Extending Democracy

We all like to think that we live in democratic societies, but our societies often fall far short of the democratic ideal. Where local government is weak, communities have little say over the character of their local areas, or about the shape and direction of the local economy. Despite the existence of local democratic institutions, and the occurrence of regular local elections, people often feel, rightly, that they lack meaningful influence over the places where they live and work, instead having the sense that they and their communities are being buffeted by powerful external forces – often economic in nature – over which they have little or no collective control. This sense of powerlessness is not an accident, but a direct result of how, under neoliberalism, more and more decisions have been removed from the sphere of democratic contestation and designated as narrow technical issues to be resolved by experts or left to the operations of supposedly immutable market forces.

At the core of the case for Community Wealth Building is a simple idea about the need to take democracy seriously. If we want to live in democratic societies, then we need to have democratic institutions that allow communities to shape their local economies, and to exert real control over the way in which those local economies develop over time. Treating the economy as some kind of separate technocratic domain in which the central values of a democratic society somehow do not apply is no longer good enough. On the contrary, taking democracy seriously involves being prepared to extend it deep into economic life – including into the ownership of enterprise. Under neoliberalism, economic thinking colonised too many of our democratic institutions; in going beyond neoliberalism to a society fit for us all to live in, we need to move in the opposite direction, orchestrating the decolonisation of our democratic institutions and their reconstruction on the basis of genuinely democratic values and practices.

Community Wealth Building is about people coming together collectively as democratic citizens to exert control over some of the most fundamental aspects of their shared life within their communities – such as employment conditions, investment, and the direction for future economic development. By combining the economic power of local government itself with the associated power of local anchor institutions such as universities, hospitals, and other public and quasi-public institutions, Community Wealth Building is an approach that looks for ways in which the collective institutions that we already have can reorient their impact on local economies.

The aim of this process of democratic expression is to shift the position of individual citizens from being bystanders, who can only watch economic forces play out in their local communities, to active participants, who can collectively give some form and direction to the economic future of their local area. At the heart of this strategy is the promotion of alternative models of ownership, whether worker cooperatives, land trusts, or forms of local public enterprise accountable to the community and under collective democratic control.[6]

The democratic argument for Community Wealth Building is a direct and powerful one. It is about creating a shift in the balance of power in determining the fate of local communities: a shift from the impersonal logic of the market to the democratic power of political institutions. It is about extending the writ of democratic decision-making within those local communities, thereby opening up space for those communities to do more to determine the shape of their own futures.

It is impossible to have a fully democratic society when the scope of democratic agency is excessively restricted, and when the day-to-day experience of living and working in society undermines rather than supports and advances one's sense of oneself as an active democratic citizen. Writing as long ago as 1848, in his *Principles of Political Economy*, John Stuart Mill argued that a more democratic economy could be seen as a precondition for a more robustly democratic society, as only if workers had the opportunity to exercise judgement and control at work would they be able to develop the kind of 'active character' on which our political institutions rely for their proper functioning.[7] As Mill put it, 'a democratic constitution, not supported by democratic institutions in detail, but confined to central government, not only is not political freedom, but often creates a spirit precisely the reverse, carrying down to the lowest grade in society the desire and ambition of political domination'.[8]

This line of argument has been extended since Mill by a tradition in political theory that passes through the guild socialism of G. D. H. Cole to the more recent radical defences of participatory democracy advanced by writers such as Carole Pateman and Joshua Cohen.[9] What these theorists of democracy have in common is the sense that the democratic citizen does not somehow exist beyond or outside the organisation of economic activity, but that questions of political and economic democracy are intimately related to one another. Joshua Cohen talks in terms of the *psychological support* that a more democratic economy can provide for democratic citizens, in creating the conditions in which individuals can develop the outlook and capacities needed to take a full role in democratic participation. 'The psychological support argument holds that the extension of self-government into the traditionally undemocratic sphere of work contributes to both the formation of an active character and to the development of a sense of the common good, and thus contributes to a more fully democratic state.'[10]

The democratic case for Community Wealth Building can be developed along similar lines to those advanced by these theories of participatory democracy. We can say that, in allowing more

scope for the collective direction of the local economy, we thereby honour the value of democracy
in two distinct ways. In a very direct way, policies
of Community Wealth Building take local people
seriously as active democratic citizens through the
provision of opportunities for democratic action in
the local economy. But while this can be valuable
in itself, there is also a less direct justification that
emphasises the role of more local and participatory forms of democratic agency as providing the
preconditions for a more democratic society at the
national level.

A Society of Equals

Although democratic values should be central to
how we think about shaping a more human model
of the economy, the case for Community Wealth
Building is not grounded solely in the value of
democracy; alongside this runs an appeal to the
value of equality. The aspiration of Community
Wealth Building is not just that communities come
to take democratic control of their local economies, but that they can come to use that control
deliberately to shape those economies in a more
egalitarian direction. At the simplest level this may

mean – for example, through the introduction of living wage policies – that there come to be more decent jobs within local economies, and that the scourge of badly paid and exploitative employment is reduced. But the operative idea of equality here is a broader one, and not confined merely to questions of economic distribution. This conception of equality encompasses an idea of what it would be to live together *as equals*: an egalitarian society isn't just one in which the material gap between the haves and the have-nots is reduced, it's also a society in which the *social* distance between the advantaged and the disadvantaged is compressed, and in which everyone can share a common life as citizens.[11]

When a local authority moves away – as some 77 per cent of UK councils are planning to do, according to the Association for Public Service Excellence (APSE) – from contracting out public services to the lowest bidder, with those services perhaps having been provided by a large multinational corporation working to an extractive model of profit maximisation and with scant concern for the development of its workers, and brings those services back in-house, paying its workers better wages and offering more in the way of voice, respect, training, and development, this can be an egalitarian transformation in more than one way.[12] It's not just that those employed in local services should be paid decently, it is also of great significance when the relationship between workers and their employers is put on a more respectful footing, and when public funds are no longer used to subsidise the extractive model of firms that make their profits in part through keeping workers voiceless, disengaged, and subject to the whims of neoliberal employment practices such as zero-hour contracts.

A more economically activist local authority, working with other local anchor institutions, can pursue the twin egalitarian ambitions of reducing both economic *and* social inequity by creating good jobs where workers have stable employment conditions, voice, and respect, as well as a decent wage. When such strategies are accompanied by efforts to create and promote new democratic economic forms such as cooperatives they can begin to transform the make-up of the private sector too, broadening ownership and control of the local and regional economy.[13]

Equality and Democracy in Local Economies

The central elements of the case for Community Wealth Building come from these twin political hopes – that is, the aspiration that we might by our collective efforts come to inhabit a society that is both more democratic and more equal. But these twin hopes are not merely fellow travellers. Rather, they are closely related to one another, and mutually reinforcing.

A more egalitarian society, with reduced social distance, more of a shared common life, and less of the domination, insecurity, and instability characteristic of the worst aspects of the neoliberal economy, is a society that creates the preconditions for a healthy and flourishing democracy.[14] Democracy cannot take firm root in a society where economic hopelessness undermines a sense of political agency, where deep social inequalities make citizens into mutual strangers, and where economic instability precludes active determination of a community's economic development, making the ambition to shape our collective future seem unattainable and sapping the attention and energy that citizens need in order to exert themselves politically.[15]

At the same time, when we come together as communities that are prepared to project our political will into the economic domain we are able to create the material preconditions of an egalitarian society.[16] Only when we extend democracy's reach can we transform according to our values the structures of day-to-day productive life, and the nature of the personal relationships to which those structures give rise, so that we can achieve a society that embodies and expresses our equal standing as citizens.[17] In other words, a more democratic economy and society help us to create the structures that allow us to live together as equals. And only when we relate as equals do we have the preconditions for flourishing democracy. The values of equality and democracy, though distinct, are intimately related.

Community Wealth Building is the institutional means by which local communities can break into this virtuous circle of mutual support and reinforcement. The aim is to forge paths towards the creation of a local economy that is both more conducive to citizens relating as equals, and which sustains citizens' standing as members of an active democracy. In doing this, the hope is that we are able to move away from a world where people are forced to exist within alienating and dehumanising economic structures, and towards a world where the economy can play a positive role in sustaining our shared life as democratic citizens.

Responding to Critiques of Community Wealth Building

The positive case for Community Wealth Building, then, goes right to the heart of our shared values of social justice, equality, and democracy. We have argued for a shift in the role of local government from that of a mere market participant, driven only by a concern for cost reduction in the provision of services, to that of a more far-seeing public institution, with a concern for the creation of the social conditions for a more egalitarian and participatory society. This shift is fundamental, as it takes the sharedness and the 'publicness' of our democratic institutions seriously, and refuses to sacrifice our common political values to the one-eyed obsessions of a dogmatic neoliberalism that is incapable of recognising value anywhere except in the economic bottom line.[18]

But what then could be said against this approach to thinking about local government? As one might expect, the main lines of critique come from a position that accepts what we might think of as a more 'neoliberal' – or, at the very least, a more 'economistic' – framing of how we should think about the role of government.[19] One line of critique accuses Community Wealth Building of being a form of self-defeating 'municipal protectionism'; a second worries about 'rent extraction' and capture by special interests; while a third is sceptical of whether citizens have the appetite or ability to play a broader role in participating in a more democratic economy. We consider each in turn below.

On Prisoner's Dilemmas, Zero-Sum Games, and 'Municipal Protectionism'

At the heart of what we might call 'the economists' critique' of Community Wealth Building is the claim that this kind of approach amounts to a form of beggar-thy-neighbour municipal protectionism. The idea here is that Community Wealth Building undermines the possibility of 'gains from trade' between different municipalities or different parts of the country. The argument is that, as procurement spending is localised, there may be a short-run benefit to the locality, but this will be at the expense of others elsewhere. And so even if Community Wealth Building can be a rational strategy for one municipality to pursue, at least in the short run, its longer-run consequences will be that, once the strategy spreads more broadly, everyone will be left worse off, as each area cuts itself off from economically attractive trading opportunities with everywhere else.

In effect, if this analysis were correct, we would be in a situation with the structure of a Prisoner's Dilemma, or what the philosopher Derek Parfit called an 'Each-We Dilemma',[20] where a particular kind of action may be to the benefit of a particular agent – in this case, a particular municipality – but the same strategy when widely adopted would be collectively self-defeating, leading, in this case, to a damaging levelling-down of economic prospects.[21] This way of thinking about local economic spending imagines a set of different municipalities engaged in what is essentially a zero-sum game, with any benefit to one region or city straightforwardly amounting to an equivalent loss experienced elsewhere.

One version of this 'municipal protectionism' critique was voiced by *The Economist* in an October 2017 piece looking at the possible significance of the Preston Model in encapsulating a new approach to economic policy. Having considered the positive reception of Preston's new approach to local public spending, *The Economist* found a commentator advancing a more critical line:

Not all are so impressed. Getting institutions to buy locally amounts to municipal protectionism, with money that was once spent elsewhere in Britain spent locally, points out Colin Talbot, a public-policy expert at Cambridge University. 'There is no value being added', he says. An overly confined economy may reduce economies of scale and exacerbate the effects of any downturn. If the Park Hotel [a local hotel development being funded through the municipal pension scheme] goes under, it may hit Preston's pensioners, too.'[22]

Substantially the same point comes up again in a later *Economist* article, on the range of ideas in leftist and progressive political economy coalescing under the broad label of 'Corbynomics'. Here is the analysis from its May 2018 piece, 'Corbynomics: The Great Transformation', which takes seriously the idea that Community Wealth Building is a way to 'take back control', but then offers an argument against the acceptance of these kinds of policies:

Buying local, as Preston does, is protectionist, a bit like banning imports. A local supplier may win a contract over a better one in the next-door town. If every council did this, Britain as a whole would be poorer. ...

These are the questions to ask of Corbynomics. And Labour's critics should keep in mind the philosophical underpinnings of these policies. As far as their supporters are concerned, criticising the plans for their inefficiency misses the point. Just as warnings that Brexit would make people poorer failed to deter those who longed to claw back power from Brussels, those same arguments against Mr Corbyn's programme may not persuade voters determined to 'take back control' of the economy.[23]

There are at least three broad ways in which one can resist this line of argument. One response is to take seriously the point acknowledged here by *The Economist*, that economic efficiency is not the only value, and that there can be good non-material reasons for favouring a particular policy even if it is not the policy that would be chosen on purely economic criteria. A second response is to emphasise distributive considerations, and to point out that in many cases a set of policies that reduce inequality, or redistribute the benefits of certain economic activities, can be justifiable even when they involve some aggregate economic loss. A third line of response is to go right to the core of this argument on its own terms, taking issue with the (often unargued) assumptions that there is no 'value added' through Community Wealth Building, and that local economic strategies simply involve local municipalities engaging in a zero-sum game.

These three lines of counter-objection are, so to speak, of increasing strength, as they are decreasingly concessive towards the kind of economistic critique that we're considering. We consider them in turn.

Non-material Benefits of Community Wealth Building: In other words, it's not just about the money. The central argument of this chapter is that we have decisive non-material reasons to want to change the character of local economies. Our fundamental claim is that we have good reason to value social equality, democracy and participation, and a more just society. If bringing about a more democratic and egalitarian society entails certain moderate economic costs, then those costs are likely to be well worth paying. It is therefore in one sense no objection whatsoever to Community Wealth Building to point out that policies that are justified when we admit a full range of pertinent values are not necessarily the policies that would be justified if we artificially limited ourselves to appealing only to the single austere value of economic efficiency.

To render this point vivid, consider an example. Imagine a local council – let's call it 'Neoliberal City Council' – that buys most of its services from an outside contractor. This contractor employs workers on zero-hour contracts, makes no effort to train them or to invest in their skills and capacities, treats those workers with ongoing disrespect, and gives them no voice in their workplaces or sense of agency in their work. Let us assume that, despite these crushingly poor employment conditions, services get provided adequately (or at least minimally) well in this area, and at low cost. Council tax is kept low. Economic efficiency is pursued. But at what cost?

It will be scant consolation to those local residents who work for the outsourcing company that their council tax levels are being kept down, if the price for that is a world in which they feel constantly marginalised, disrespected, and side-lined, and where their precarious employment conditions make life unpredictable and demoralising, with long-term planning almost impossible. And this is not even to touch upon the kind of democratic spill-over effects from a more participatory society that are discussed by political theorists such as John Stuart Mill, Carole Pateman, and Joshua Cohen, and which would be entirely missing in a local economy full of such dreadful, deadening jobs.

The Economist is therefore right to suggest that criticising economic policies for their inefficiency, without considering whether purely economic inefficiencies are outbalanced by important gains of other kinds, is beside the point. However, to radicalise this line of argument, it is important to note that it does not depend on a peculiar normative orientation shared only by those predisposed to accept leftist policies, as *The Economist* seems to imply with its qualifying phrase 'as far as their supporters are concerned'. The point is that absolutely *any* plausible view of public policy has to allow that there is a multiplicity of values, of which economic efficiency is merely one (even if it is an important value within this broader range).

Not to acknowledge this elementary truth is to back oneself into a rather grim corner where one is capable of knowing only the price of everything and the value of nothing. It can never be a sufficient objection to some policy simply to point out that it carries certain economic costs compared with other alternatives, or indeed that it is deficient with regard to any one particular value or desiderata, without then engaging in the more important assessment of whether, all things considered, that loss or cost is justifiable when measured against the concomitant benefits of doing things differently.

Justice, Distribution, and Conceptions of Efficiency: The previous counter-objection is an important one, but to rely on it too heavily would be to give away too much ground. If all we were saying in defence of Community Wealth Building was that it involves trading off economic costs against the less tangible gains in terms of equality and democracy, then we would be making a solid and justifiable point, while also constructing a dialectical situation that is too comfortable for the critics of Community Wealth Building and for the defenders of the neo-liberal status quo. It suits a neoliberal outlook to pretend that the case for radical economic policies is always about the promotion of fuzzier and less tangible values against the concrete benefits of eco-nomic good sense. Thankfully, although we stand behind the counter-argument given above in terms of the non-material benefits of Community Wealth Building, we do not think that this is the only line of support available, and hence it is important to defend the importance of non-material benefits and values without ceding too much ground on economic questions to the defenders of a neoliberal policy approach.

One way of making the justificatory story more complicated is to bring in distributive considera-tions. It is one thing to say that a particular policy promotes economic efficiency, or creates economic value, but something else entirely to then raise the question of where the gains of efficiency are allocated within an economic system. Let's go back to our imagined case of Neoliberal City Council. Imagine that its outsourcing contractors are so good at driving down the costs of service provision, including the wages of their workers, that they are able to extract strong levels of profit from their council contracts. In one sense this looks like a paradigm case of an efficient system, if the cost to the council for service provision is lower than it otherwise would have been, and the benefits of cutting costs can then be shared (albeit probably not evenly) between council-tax payers and the outsourcing company itself.

But our thinking about such a situation is likely to change when we consider that workers are not *just* a cost to be minimised, as we might want to minimise the costs of heating or lighting or transportation. Workers are also citizens, both locally and nationally, and as such they are owed justification for the policies that are enacted by their democratic institutions, and which affect them so profoundly and pervasively. Moreover, workers – unlike the other 'inputs' into production – are individuals for whom things can go better or worse, and whose welfare can be higher or lower. And because workers are not merely a cost of production, there are two perspectives from which to think about wage levels: the perspective of those receiving those wages and the perspective of those bearing the costs of those wages. A policy of relentlessly driving down costs in service provision by reducing wages can therefore be seen to raise serious and unignorable distributive questions.

To put things simply and directly, a loss of efficiency looks much less decisive – even when we confine ourselves to economic terms rather than straying onto a broader normative terrain – when we bear in mind issues of distribution. If thousands of council workers (who in general will also be local citizens) are left significantly worse off by virtue of a policy of outsourcing that may bring only small benefits in cost reduction for local citizens, while primarily benefitting the outsourcing companies and their shareholders, then it seems like a very weak claim – even in purely economic terms – to emphasise the significance of a gain in overall efficiency. Some cost-reducing changes of policy have their primary economic effects through leaving workers much worse off while increasing returns to firms and to their owners, driving up levels of inequality in the process.[24]

This line of argument illustrates the bizarre ways in which the idea of efficiency gets used in a great deal of debate about public policy. One technical concept of efficiency used in economics is the idea of Pareto efficiency, whereby a policy or distribution is efficient when nobody can be made better off without somebody else being made worse off. A Pareto improvement, then, or a gain in Pareto efficiency, is a change in the situation that makes at least someone better off, without making anyone else worse off.[25] But changes in public policy almost *never* involve an improvement in Pareto efficiency, given that such changes nearly always have both winners *and* losers. Any large policy change is likely to affect many people in a variety of ways, placing us well outside the kind of neat formal models in which a policy can bring an uncontroversial Pareto improvement.[26] And so when we are analysing real policy changes rather than abstract hypothetical cases, it's (almost) never the strict sense of Pareto efficiency that is in play when we talk about economic efficiency.

In our imagined case, the outsourcing policies of Neoliberal City Council that drive down staff costs and reduce council-tax bills, while benefitting the outsourcing company and leaving workers worse off, would obviously not constitute a gain in Pareto efficiency, precisely because there is an identifiable group (the workers) who are left worse off. Of course, what is usually being appealed to in talk of 'economic efficiency' is not the idea of Paretian efficiency but some broader idea of increasing aggregate output or aggregate economic activity. To relate changes in aggregate economic levels to a notion of economic efficiency, economists have recourse to the idea of Kaldor-Hicks efficiency, named after its intellectual progenitors Nicholas Kaldor and John Hicks.[27] A change in policy increases efficiency in the Kaldor-Hicks sense when those who are made better off by the change *could* in principle compensate those who had been made worse off, so that a Pareto superior distribution *could* be accessible given the requisite degree of redistribution of the benefits. In our case, we could say that the shift to outsourcing in Neoliberal City would involve a gain in terms of Kaldor-Hicks efficiency if the savings to the council-tax payers and the profits of the outsourcing company were sufficiently large to compensate for the losses to the workers whose wages had been cut.

Let us imagine a situation where, in these terms, there really is an efficiency gain from outsourcing (in Kaldor-Hicks terms), because the change in service provision creates an economic surplus that can, at least in principle, be redistributed to those, i.e. the workers, who have lost out from the change. What is important to grasp here is that there is all the difference in the world between achieving an economic gain that *could* be redistributed and achieving an economic gain that actually *is* redistributed. When the redistribution is merely possible, but not actual, it is difficult to see why the normative appeal of increasing efficiency should be so compelling to those who lose out from those efficiency gains.

Staying with our example, let's imagine that in actual fact the lion's share of the gains go to the outsourcing company's already well-off senior management and shareholders. Redistribution perhaps *could* leave nobody worse off, but this redistribution does not in fact occur, and therefore what we have is a situation with winners and losers, where the winners are already relatively well-off and the losers are already among the more disadvantaged. Even if we don't think there are independent reasons, such as the social egalitarian reasons discussed earlier in this chapter, to reduce overall levels of inequality, it is not hard to see that policies that bring aggregate economic gains while nevertheless leaving many people worse off are not policies that would reasonably command the support of those who do not directly benefit from them.

So much economic discourse about economic efficiency in fact operates by a kind of sleight-of-hand: it carries the normative authority of an idea of efficiency that it would seem unreasonable not to treat seriously – that is, the Paretian idea of benefitting some while leaving nobody worse off – and then tries to carry that normative authority across into contexts where Paretian efficiency is not achieved, but where we simply have policy changes that involve winners and losers. A policy that brings Kaldor-Hicks improvements in a context where no compensatory redistribution will in fact take place, where shareholders and senior managers make a killing but workers are left short-changed, is not a policy that most people have good reasons to support *even in narrow economic terms*. This point applies clearly in the context of Community Wealth Building, especially given the need to integrate the perspective of workers-as-citizens, instead of getting stuck on a conception of workers-as-cost, but it also has broader relevance across our thinking in many areas of public policy. We should not accept a kind of 'halo' effect for judgements of greater economic efficiency when the form of efficiency in question would only leave everyone better off if policies of compensatory redistribution were in place – policies that in fact aren't being either planned or considered.[28]

The Direct Economic Case for Community Wealth Building: Efficiency, Economic Systems, and Resisting Extraction: The previous counter-objection made the important point that a policy may not be justifiable even when it increases economic efficiency in the weak sense of advancing aggregate output. Our third line of response to the economistic critique goes deeper, pointing out that in many cases Community Wealth Building policies will actually be better even in terms of aggregate economic returns. This can happen in a number of ways. What they have in common is that the ways in which economistic objections to Community Wealth Building can fail in general become clearer when we take a broader and more systemic perspective. As above, we need to remember that workers are citizens, as well as a cost of production, and that citizens have their own particular histories and hopes for the future, with ties to particular places. When we make the shift from the abstraction of austere economic models to the context of real world policy-making and implementation, the case for Community Wealth Building only becomes stronger, and the economists' counter-objections even less plausible. Here, then, are four ways in which the economistic or neoliberal case against Community Wealth Building can fail entirely, when we shift to a suitably broad view of the functioning of the economy:

(a) A first point is that, by encouraging a shift to better employment practices, we may be increasing the costs of production and service provision, but we are also investing in the future. A local council that includes requirements that contractors invest in their employees' skills and development, or which ensures that its contractors provide training and apprenticeships, is making a good value investment in the local labour force, an investment that will likely bear significant returns over time, and which would never be made in a world of low-quality employment opportunities and zero-hour contracts. Taking a longer-run, more systemic perspective, it is likely that an approach to employment that treats workers as worthy of long-term investment, rather than treating them as a disposable cheap input, will maximise the productive potential, and hence the aggregate economic output, of the economy as a whole.

(b) A second point, made by Thad Williamson, David Imbroscio, and Gar Alperovitz in *Making a Place for Community: Local Democracy in a Global Era*, emphasises the idea of the embedded costs of place – both human and physical – and the idea of the local public balance sheet. As societies, we have embedded enormous collective investments into the physical and social infrastructure of our cities. Therefore any economic strategy that does not take seriously the fact that institutions are already in place, and that people already treat particular localities as their long-term homes, is going to countenance a 'throw-away' approach to certain cities or localities that is as damaging in economic terms as it is in human terms. This comes back to the point that humans are real, have lives and histories, and aren't just a fungible cost of production. As Williamson et al. put it:

> the traditional efficiency argument against place-based economic policy is fundamentally flawed ... [as] it fails to take account of the costs of what we term 'throw-away cities' ... as well as the sunk private and public investments in infrastructure, housing, commercial buildings, education, utilities, and other public goods that are left to decay or are abandoned outright (while those very same structures, goods and services must be provided in other communities).[29]

The fate of a Cleveland or a Detroit is not only a disaster in terms of the non-material costs of shattering communities, it is also a grotesque economic waste in purely material terms. An approach myopically focused on the costs of particular policies at the margin will fail to take the systemic perspective that renders this point visible, despite the fact that, as soon as one takes a broader and longer-run economic view, the wastefulness of not accounting for the social and institutional inheritances of particular places is patently absurd.

(c) A third point is in some senses the obverse of the foregoing point. It is that, just as a developing country might reasonably make short-term use of 'protectionist' policies in order to promote local multipliers as a way of boosting its own progress along its development path (as economists such as Ha-Joon Chang have convincingly argued),[30] so too there may be a case for similar action at a municipal level. Formal arguments against 'local protectionism' often assume that all the areas in question are operating at similar levels of economic output relative to their capacity, or all have full employment. But when one particular municipality has a local 'output gap', the short-run use of local development policies that deliberately utilise local multipliers can be a rational and prudent strategy.

(d) Fourthly, again taking a broader perspective, it is worth thinking not so much about local multipliers as about where in the system we find the form of pure economic 'extraction' associated with corporate tax avoidance.[31] Consider the choice between a large international outsourcing company that is very good at skilfully minimising its tax liabilities, and hence is an efficient 'extractor' of economic value, and a local supplier that meets its full tax obligations in a more straightforward way, duly paying a proportion of its profits back into the public purse. The case for always focusing on upfront marginal costs obviously fades significantly when we shift to a more systemic perspective that sets those costs against the tax practices of the contractors in question.[32]

Rent Extraction, Capture by Special Interests, and the Alleged Impossibility of Democracy

Alongside the 'municipal protectionism' critique that we have been concerned to rebut above, there's a parallel strand to the economists' critique of Community Wealth Building that is less concerned with the allegedly self-defeating logic of each city or municipality being especially concerned with the advancement of its own local economy, and instead is motivated by a broader scepticism about the very possibility of having a more democratic economic system. The argument here is that, as soon as one departs from decision-making made purely on the basis of narrowly defined economic criteria, and instead finds space for genuine democratic agency within local authorities' decision-making in the economic domain, then one somehow opens the door to a free-for-all in which cronyism and rent extraction will proliferate. Here's *The Economist* again:

> The bigger question-mark over Labour's plans to 'democratise' the economy is whether they would really put ordinary people in charge. Distant, out-of-touch private managers could simply be replaced by distant, out-of-touch public bosses or by party apparatchiks. Removing the focus on economic returns might make it easier to justify doling out jobs or contracts to political allies.[33]

One can allow that this raises an important issue while resisting the apparent assumption that there is a stark choice to be made between either an impeccably efficient economistic focus on marginal cost to the exclusion of everything else, or a more democratic approach somehow bound to degenerate into cronyism. There are of course other possibilities, and there are ways of protecting procurement processes from abuse. It is clear even from the UK's existing 2012 Social Value Act that conceptually there is nothing unattainable about having transparent and auditable procurement criteria that go beyond consideration only of marginal economic cost.

But the broader point here is that we need to guard against the besetting vice of a certain kind of economistic outlook which is concerned always to compare an idealised or perfect version of neoliberal capitalism (rather than its less savoury reality) against a non-idealised or dysfunctional version of an alternative system. (Of course, we should also guard against the opposite tendency.) One can, and should, admit that rent-seeking and 'corporate capture' are real problems for any economic system, without being too quick to find the mote in the eye of the democratic economy while ignoring the beam in the eye of neoliberalism. One has only to look at the operations of outsourcing companies like Capita or Carillion in the UK to see how traditional approaches to procurement have led to an extravaganza of failure and rent extraction.[34]

Clarity in procedures, and probity in their application, can certainly be achieved under a more democratic economy and, in fact, the more democratic engagement and scrutiny that can be generated, the more likely such outcomes are to be realised. As for *The Economist*'s worry that a democratic local economy may end up being insufficiently democratic, far from being a critique of the idea of economic democracy, it actually amounts to a recommendation that such policies be pursued either in their radical and ambitious versions or not at all. We are happy to take that as a welcome recommendation.

Too Many Meetings? 'The Problem With Socialism is That it Takes Too Many Evenings'

Oscar Wilde, the author of *The Soul of Man Under Socialism*, understood well the relationship between economic institutions and the inner lives of those living under and within those institutions.[35] He put his finger on one potential problem of more democratic forms of collective organisation when he famously quipped (although the attribution may be apocryphal) that 'the problem with socialism is that it takes too many evenings'. In our terms, the worry would be that a more democratic economy might make unrealisable demands on the citizens who will be its participants. There are two responses to this Wildean line of critique; responses that are individually strong, and jointly decisive. The first is that one should not overestimate what would be required – not endless participation in economic decision-making by all of the people all of the time, but only participation by some of the people some of the time. Even extremely successful democratic enterprises such as Mondragón in Spain do not expect or require endless engagement by all worker-owners in every forum, only that there will be a spectrum of engagement sufficient for a critical level of participation.[36]

The other line of response is that, just as one should not overestimate what is required in citizens' and workers' participation in a more democratic economy, neither should one underestimate the capacities of one's fellow citizens. When people have real power to affect matters that are central to their lives as economic agents, it would be entirely reasonable to expect a level of engagement much higher than what one could expect in contexts where people are powerless. And if there is a guiding idea behind 'the institutional turn' in the political economy of the left it is that we should not consider people's motives and outlooks in isolation from the institutions that shape their lives, but think carefully about how such institutions create beliefs, motives, and perceptions. As with the previous objection, the most natural conclusion to draw from considering this line of possible critique of the democratic economy is that the biggest danger is excessive caution, and the most plausible policies will be those that create opportunities for the dispersal of real power to citizens and workers.

Conclusion:
Building Democratic and Egalitarian Local Economies

Our central normative claim, then, is that there is a desperate need to respond to the multiple crises of neoliberalism by taking the collective decision to forge an economy that is both more equal and more broadly participatory. We make the case that there is a close relation at two levels between equality and democracy, with these two political values being intertwined at the level of theory, while also running in a relation of close mutual support at the level of institutional realisation. Community Wealth Building is a central, crucial, and emblematic means of realising just such an economy. But since it is only part of a broader picture, in our concluding chapter we turn to the question of the place of Community Wealth Building within a wider ecosystem of economic transformation.

3

Community Wealth Building and the Institutional Turn: Routes to a Democratic Economy

In this final chapter we move beyond the immediate application and justification for Community Wealth Building to take up the question of the role it can play in the transition towards a more just economic system beyond neoliberal capitalism. We consider how current democratic experiments in Community Wealth Building might be scaled-up and generalised as part of a new political-economic settlement on both sides of the Atlantic. At the time of writing, the most immediate opportunities are likely in the United Kingdom via the policy and political platform of the British Labour Party being developed at present under the leadership of Jeremy Corbyn and John McDonnell. But whatever the shape of future political developments, whenever our societies become able to move beyond the limits of the current failed model of neoliberalism, Community Wealth Building can form a central part of that movement towards something better.

At the core of this new approach is a set of models, institutions, and strategies that, if put in place, would in and of themselves produce vastly improved societal outcomes. We start from the premise that if powerful underlying trends are to be altered it is no longer possible to sidestep fundamental questions of ownership and control, and conclude that, ultimately, a truly impactful alternative strategy must democratise capital itself. Instead of the extractive and concentrating forces of corporate capitalism, our next system will need to be circulatory and place-based, decentralising economic power, rebuilding and stabilising regions and local communities, allowing for the possibility of real democracy and participation, and providing the long-run institutional and policy support for a new politics dedicated to achieving genuine ecological sustainability and social change.

The stakes could hardly be much higher. In the face of what is clearly a growing systemic crisis – encompassing deepening social and environmental calamities and a decaying neoliberal economic model that continues to generate dangerous inequalities of wealth and power – this bold but practical agenda for a renewed twenty-first-century socialism is one of the few bright spots in an otherwise forbiddingly bleak international scene. With a far-right backlash against the existing order evident from Italy to India, and from the United States to Brazil, much will depend on how and whether this fledgling approach can be further developed and advanced and taken to full scale and impact over the coming years. As a left alternative to both extractive neoliberalism and xenophobic nationalism, and as an agenda that is capable of being taken up and rapidly implemented, it looks at present to be the only game in town. With the successes of the Preston Model, and the British Labour Party's commitment to the development of Community Wealth Building in local government, the United Kingdom is at the very tip of the spear globally in bringing this radical new economic approach to the threshold of national-level state power.

Principles of a Democratic Economy: The Need for Systemic Change

Community Wealth Building represents in microcosm a new approach to a more democratic economy. We can see this by looking at some of the principles of Community Wealth Building that have been identified by its theorists and practitioners. The Democracy Collaborative offers eight principles:

- The priority of *labour over capital*, particularly in a crisis, with continued stable employment more important than capital's profits.
- The need for *local and broad-based ownership* rather than absentee ownership, as the basis for asserting what interests are valued.
- The importance of *active democratic ownership* contrasted with the passive, consumer model of neoliberalism.
- The central role for *multipliers* and internalising the circulation of money, with investment sticking rather than capital being extracted.
- Economic development understood not as a partnership between the state and business, in which the state is unaccountable and subordinate, but as a *multi-stakeholder process*.
- *Place matters*, and direct investment in neighbourhoods, particularly neighbourhoods of colour, is necessary, as 'trickle down' into these neighbourhoods in particular cannot be relied upon.
- *Systemic change* is the long-term goal, since the current system destroys the environment and

produces inequalities, making it necessary to move beyond amelioration to build systems that produce different outcomes.

These principles suggest a degree of ambition for the Community Wealth Building agenda that carries it far beyond a local-level alternative to the prevailing model of community economic development. Looking beyond the local, the approach embodied in these principles begins to sketch and advance a comprehensive economic alternative to neoliberalism.

As we argued in Chapter 1, deepening systemic problems – climate change, economic stagnation, disinvestment, racial and gender disparities, widening inequalities of wealth and power – are not simply accidental or the result of poor policy choices. Rather, they are the entirely predictable outcomes of the basic organisation of our economic system. The institutional arrangements at the heart of today's neoliberal capitalism drive the outcomes we are seeing in terms of crumbling public infrastructure, environmental destruction, social atomisation, and a widespread sense of popular disempowerment. Our system is programmed not to meet basic needs but to steadily concentrate virtually all economic gains in the hands of a tiny super-elite at huge social and environmental cost. If we are serious about addressing our real challenges then we need a different set of institutions and arrangements capable of producing sustainable, lasting, and more democratic outcomes as a matter of course – a genuine 'next system'. There is thus an urgent need for a pluralist vision of a new type of economy centred on the values lacking in the current system.

Such a vision, as we have argued, can begin by drawing upon a myriad of local and municipal experiments in democratised ownership, community control, and revitalised local economies – a deep and growing base of practical experience in our new 'laboratories of democracy'. These models begin to prefigure and, critically, can help clarify the contours of the much larger-scale solutions that are ultimately needed for a wholesale reordering of such major economic systems as finance, trade, planning, regulation, and democratic decision-making at the regional, national, and – ultimately – international levels.

We are faced with a crisis of our political-economic system on multiple levels, from the looming threat of ecological collapse due to climate change to the massive political backlash that is already building against what Karl Polanyi termed the 'stark utopia' of the universalisation of the market as the governing principle of social organisation – a backlash which could and already is taking both radical left and far right forms.[1] The struggle is already underway as to which side will provide the most politically salient and saleable responses and thereby take the field. With the newly emerging political economy of Community Wealth Building we find the best contender yet from the left that could be capable of winning the day. We had better hope it is up to the task, as the alternatives do not bear thinking about. To quote Dee Ward Hock, 'It's far too late and things are far too bad for pessimism.'

Returns to Capital

Who owns and controls capital – productive wealth – is among the most fundamental questions of political economy, central to understanding the operations of any economic system. For socialists, responses to capitalist private ownership of the economy have traditionally divided along two main lines. In greatly simplified terms, *state socialism* placed ownership and control of capital with the state, whereas *social democracy* left it largely in private hands but sought to redistribute the returns through taxation and transfers. A neglected third tradition, however, largely eclipsed by the left's great twentieth-century projects, is to be found in the long-running socialist commitment to *economic democracy*.

In *A Preface to Economic Democracy*, Robert Dahl defined economic democracy as 'help[ing] to strengthen political equality and democracy by reducing inequalities originating in the ownership and control of firms'.[2] Approaching the question from the opposite end, G. D. H. Cole, the British socialist theorist and advocate of economic democracy, argued that principles of democracy should apply 'not only or mainly to some special sphere of social action known as "politics", but to any and every form of social action, and, in especial, to industrial and economic fully as much as to political offices'.[3]

When it comes to economic fundamentals, there has been a decades-long deficit of new thinking and ideas on the left. Where they have not capitulated totally to neoliberalism, most social democrats have been splashing around far downstream from where the real action is, seeking a way forward through 'tax and spend' transfer policies and modest redistribution. This has been true even of some of the most creative interventions. Thomas Piketty, for instance, in his best-selling book *Capital in the Twenty-First Century* – a masterwork of statistical analysis of capital accumulation that demonstrated capitalism's 'fundamental force for divergence' – largely avoided grappling with the deep structural determinants of who owns capital, focusing instead on the distant prospect of 'regulating capital' via a global wealth tax. But given that returns to capital are increasing at the expense of labour's share, and that automation threatens to accelerate these trends, it's only natural that we should be looking at broadening and democratising ownership.[4] Nobel Laureate Robert Solow commented to this effect during a 2014 panel on Piketty's book in Washington, DC. Among the 'things we can do', Solow observed, 'democratising the ownership of wealth is perhaps the most obvious'.

As we have seen, none of this is about selling a fantasy. Real-world examples of democratic, participatory economic alternatives exist in communities across the globe. Worker ownership, cooperatives, municipal enterprise, land trusts, public banks, and a host of kindred institutional forms all represent ways in which capital can be held in common by both small and large publics. They illuminate how practical new approaches can generate innovative solutions to deep underlying problems. They embody alternative design principles, relying not on regulatory fixes or 'after the fact' redistribution but on fundamental structural changes in the economy. These structural changes to the nature of ownership and control over productive wealth go right to the heart of our current difficulties – and are capable of producing greatly improved distributional and other outcomes. These institutional alternatives breathe new life into old traditions of economic democracy through the democratisation of wealth.[5]

The challenge of the present era of pain and difficulty requires a decisive political response. It is no use, when addressing civilisational problems, from climate change to runaway inequality, adopting a defensive posture, fighting a rearguard action on ever less favourable terrain. Traditional liberal and social democratic strategies to achieve equitable and sustainable outcomes simply no longer work in altering most of the big trends. Governments of all political complexions have lacked both the will and the capacity to use taxation and redistribution to significantly reduce inequality or to regulate corporations effectively. Puttering around on the edge of the impending climate catastrophe, we fail to understand that we face a system-wide crisis, not simply an economic and political crisis.

Adequately responding to this crisis calls for an intellectual confidence and a political-economic strategy capable of uniting a broad coalition around a shared agenda for building power. The aim should be that of mobilising the potential mass movement for fundamental transformation that is clearly in the making, which requires the development of new alliances that are necessary to bring about lasting change. Traditional American liberalism and European social democracy depended upon trade union strength at a level that is unlikely simply to reappear. A new economy will require new power bases rooted in new institutions and communities. Unless we are ready to offer powerful, actionable visions of shared community and mutual prosperity in opposition to the nightmares of fear, hatred, and isolation that have seized our politics, we will not win.

Moving to Large-Order Change

As we have seen, the failure of traditional politics and policies to address fundamental challenges has fuelled an extraordinary amount of experimentation in communities around the world. Practical precedents, models, and strategies already exist that build from the bottom up and begin to suggest radical new possibilities. Cooperatives, worker-owned companies, social enterprises, public banks, community land trusts, neighbourhood corporations, municipal enterprises, anchor institution approaches, participatory budgeting, local food systems – in a thousand different places, ordinary people have been at work creating solutions, building knowledge and power and solidarity from the ground up. As mentioned earlier, there are now more worker-owners in the United States than are members of unions in the private sector.

The full scale of the possibilities is just beginning to be understood. Public trusts – which already exist in places like Alaska and Texas, where they receive revenues from the sale of permits for mining and drilling – can be extended into additional domains, from water and air to the electromagnetic spectrum, underwriting public services or issuing a citizen dividend. Platform co-ops can offer a democratic alternative to the increasingly evident depredations of the current 'sharing economy' on the model of Uber and Deliveroo. Community ownership of land can ensure the long-term affordability of housing and prevent disruptive gentrification and speculative real estate bubbles. Participatory budgeting and planning approaches can establish local democratic control over the allocation and distribution of public funds.

There is a powerful agenda here for further inquiry and exploration, built around a framework of policy and structural reforms – 'non-reformist reforms' in André Gorz's terms[6] – that will indicate some of the major areas of research and work for an expanded and ambitious left political project. There is an emergent agenda focused on developing and popularising key conceptual resources for systemic change that can help catalyse long-term transformation, and help movements respond to key moments of opportunity in which larger-scale systemic shifts become possible if we are prepared. This would provide the growing networks of political activists on both sides of the Atlantic convinced of the necessity for systemic change with clear, actionable proposals for real alternatives.

Among the likely large-scale elements of a truly compelling national system-changing vision are the following:[7]

- *Public control of the financial system*, such that we can move away from our extractive, growth-addicted, wealth-concentrating, 100-year-old corporate-dominated money and banking system to a new, democratic, and fully public model.

Wall Street and the City of London sit atop two of the most highly financialised economies in the world, with *rentier* concerns predominating over productive investment and social need. We need a new approach that puts credit creation and investment at the service of the real economy and public priorities. Over time, the aim should be to move in the direction of a fully democratic financial model at the community, regional, and national levels. There are a host of possibilities for more democratic banking and finance, from public and postal banking systems to mutual and credit unions. We must also be ready with plans to nationalise the large corporate banks when the next financial crisis hits – as it inevitably will. A new money and banking system would allow for a more active fiscal and monetary policy to allocate credit in the economy towards social, environmental, and community development ends.

- *Democratisation of the basic institutions of economic life*, including large-scale expansion of worker and community ownership.

Slowly but surely, the attractions of worker ownership and control are creeping back up the political agenda, given their suitability as instruments for tackling inequality and allowing ordinary people to take back control over their lives and the economy as a whole. Public authorities should be actively supporting and funding the incubation and expansion of worker cooperatives linked to anchor-procurement and community building as part of their local economic development strategies. A large worker-owned and cooperative sector could form an important institutional base for a new place-based economics and politics – one that is capable of overturning simplistic notions of 'pro- or anti-business' and replacing them with new alignments around re-circulatory local economies built on multipliers in opposition to extractive multinational corporations.

- *Regional economic planning for sustainability*, including the development and implementation of a 'Green New Deal' industrial strategy to support the building and sustaining of markets and production capacities for distributed forms of green energy, transport, and technology.

In many places the challenges of post-industrial decline remain starkly present. It is time to revisit the possibilities inherent in an aggressive industrial strategy, both locally and nationally. A true community-sustaining industrial strategy would consist in the deliberate direction of capital to specific sectors, localities, and regions so as to balance out harmful market trends and prevent communities from falling into decay. In some cases this might mean assistance in allowing workers to buy up facilities and keep them running. In other cases, it might involve retraining workers for new skills and refitting facilities for work in a different industry. In either case, affected localities and populations would be able to participate in planning and to draw upon public resources whose aim is to help secure the long-term stability of community and sustain national production in key sectors and industries.

Community-sustaining policies to preserve particular places can be married to sector-based approaches. Green manufacturing strategies and services can support the building and sustaining of demand and production capacities for ecologically sustainable forms of energy and technology. An industrial strategy designed to underpin a Green New Deal could help overcome multiple economic challenges. It could provide high-wage jobs, generate revenue, expand exports, and reduce trade deficits – all while reducing carbon emissions and improving air quality and public health.

- *Democratisation of the economy at scale*, including the 'commanding heights', likely requiring large-scale national, regional, and municipal public ownership of corporations in sectors that require – for technological and other reasons – continued consolidation and vertical integration.

Increasing inequality, poverty, environmental degradation, and the catastrophic threat of climate change, together with a general sense of an impoverished public sphere and loss of economic control wrought by decades of privatisation and globalisation, are pushing activists and theorists back in the direction of public ownership. It's time to set out the role of an expanded and fundamentally reimagined public sector – from the ownership of enterprise, to the promotion of innovation, to healthcare and education and the production of knowledge.

As calls for public ownership at various scales grow, many activists and thinkers engaged in its recovery and rehabilitation have already argued against a simple return to the top-down centralised public corporation model of the postwar period. The fightback against privatisation of public services has been accompanied by the adoption of innovative new approaches to collective ownership. In this view, worker ownership, consumer cooperatives, municipal enterprise, and a host of kindred institutional forms all represent ways in which assets and enterprises can be held in common – including through hybrid models that draw upon two or more institutional forms.

In parts of Asia, Africa, and Latin America, new 'public-public partnerships' in water and other sectors herald the emergence of a more pluralistic approach to public ownership, while a wave of remunicipalisation has been occurring in more than 1,600 cities worldwide, as documented by researchers at the Transnational Institute (TNI).[8] The question at this point should not be a technical economic one about efficiency – the literature shows that public ownership is decidedly *not* inherently less efficient – but rather a political one about power, democracy, the social benefits of ownership, and which particular forms of collective enterprise we might wish to promote.

- **New regimes for managing macroeconomic and regional imbalances**, moving beyond 'peak globalisation' to a system of fair and managed trade and investment flows.

It is critical that the left begins to set out a plausible trade model, for application in both the short and longer term. This must allow for an economy considerably less exposed to the vagaries of international trade and finance, one of the areas in which the contemporary left has shown the least economic imagination. Once the preserve of the alter-globalisation movement, critiques of 'free trade' agreements, offshoring, and unrestricted capital flows have increasingly become the political property of the populist right, of Trump and his ilk, with dangerous consequences in regions ravaged by disinvestment and deindustrialisation.

What is needed is a reconceptualisation of managed trade that goes beyond archaic protection*ism* to instead provide the capacity for *actual protection* – for democratic autonomy, locally embedded economies, and the policy space required for a new approach to regional and national development. A new model of managed trade could open up the prospect of reindustrialisation, improved economic and job security, and community stability – thereby blunting the edge of right populism. It can also offer the basis for genuine solidarity with and economic support for communities in the global South.

- *Democratic planning to replace the current broken economic development model*, including spatial planning to build more sustainable and resilient communities, towns, cities, and regions.

If new democratic economic institutions are not to float helplessly in the sea of the capitalist marketplace, alternative economic strategies will likely need to include substantial planning capacities and functions. In a political context still dominated by neoliberal orthodoxy, *planning* remains an even dirtier word than *nationalisation* – even though it is widespread in the internal decision-making of large private corporations, many of which are bigger economic entities than some countries.[9] Given the pressing demands of climate change, including the radical unevenness of its impacts, the next few decades will doubtless require a considerably greater role for economic planning than has been the case in the last few decades.

Advances in technology and computational power can now sustain far more sophisticated planning systems than could be dreamt of in the twentieth century. However, experience demonstrates that such planning must be made democratic and participatory as well as effective. A starting point is the contemporary opportunity to establish and expand participatory budgeting at the municipal level, creating neighbourhood assemblies in towns, cities, and counties that can take a more robust role in charting their own economic course.[10] Another element is the empowerment of democratised municipal and regional economic planning commissions, comprised of directly elected representatives, stakeholder representatives, and representatives from local citizens' assemblies. Such a system could give real economic decision-making power to a new generation of devolved local and regional authorities.

- *Decommodification of land and housing*, as the basis for an expansion of the commons and of community control.

Land and real property ownership is, and always has been, of fundamental importance in determining the distribution of wealth and power. In many large cities, enormous pressures are being placed upon affordable land and housing by property speculation that has become synonymous with today's financialised capitalism, a phenomenon that can be viewed at its grotesque pinnacle in London's 'ghost towers' of empty luxury apartment blocks, rising above a city in which thousands live homeless on the streets.[11] At the same time, the geography of neoliberalism is creating wastelands in many regions.

Democratising the ownership of land and housing and increasing community control over urban and rural development are critical for stabilising local communities – both economically and in terms of population. We ought to encourage movement towards decommodification and a commons-based approach whereby communities can self-organise to manage and steward their own land and housing resources. There are a variety of historical examples and precedents for this approach, including community buyouts of land in Scotland, community land trusts in the United States, public housing in Vienna, and the vision and models of the tenants' movement in Britain.[12]

*

To rise to the challenge of this profoundly dangerous era of pain and difficulty means advancing a practicable alternative economics commensurate with the enormity of the task of community stabilisation, and reconstruction at the level of the nation as a whole. Prior to the 1930s, key elements of what became the New Deal were developed in America's state and local 'laboratories of democracy'. This hard work laid the ground both for new national institutions and programmes and a new national politics – a progressive vision that, at the time, offered something to hope for, to work towards, and which could counter the traditional corporate power that had dominated the preceding decades.

As the Great Depression got underway in the United States after the Wall Street Crash of 1929, the levels of economic pain and hardship grew. But the prevailing ideology of that time (not too dissimilar to that of our own neoliberal era) was that the Federal government should do nothing to address the economic cataclysm unfolding across the country. Instead, in accordance with the ideology of laissez-faire, the market would be allowed to correct itself. And so, in community after community, people were left with no alternative but to begin addressing their problems themselves. New approaches were devised that could eventually be scaled up when a new political opening presented itself in due course. America's primary social safety net for the elderly – the Social Security system – began with prototypes in Alaska and California as people grappled creatively with the deep economic challenges they were confronting. When the politics changed nationally, with the Roosevelt Administration coming to power and launching the New Deal, these small local models could then be lifted up into a comprehensive national system of support for older Americans, one that still endures today.

A similar process could be observed in Britain. When Nye Bevan launched the National Health Service in 1948, he was able to draw for inspiration upon the Tredegar Medical Aid Society, a community-based model in his hometown in South Wales where workers had banded together in a friendly society 'to provide for themselves and their families medical aid beyond the bare facilities available'.[13] Begun in 1890, this Friendly Society grew to serve the vast majority of the town's population, encompassing the services of five general practitioners, a surgeon, two pharmacists, a dentist, a physiotherapist, and a domiciliary nurse – all 'free at the point of use'.[14] When the Attlee government was elected in a landslide and Bevan set about the construction of the NHS, this small Welsh experiment could serve as an exemplar and inspiration for what would be possible at the national level, in creating one of the world's great national health systems.

Just as these major components of the post-war settlement in the United Kingdom and United States – socialised medicine and retirement security – were developed in response to pain and crisis, so today the emerging landscape of Community Wealth Building institutions and approaches offers a prefiguration of the principles, values, and design of what could become the next political-economic settlement, beyond today's decaying and crisis-prone neoliberal order.

*

In addition to building up a body of system-change ideas and strategies, there is also a need to focus much more attention on the question of specific pathways to change. Emerging social movements need much more developed plans in the struggle to build the institutions of the next system as the old system continues to decay, along with concrete strategies and designs for action that may be possible now or in moments of crisis – as, for instance, when the next major banking crisis opens up possibilities for overhauling the financial system. A strategically minded left needs to be ready for the time when the pendulum swings – in communities and localities, and ultimately nationally – by laying the groundwork for an institutionally based programme of political and economic democracy. As the Sanders and Corbyn phenomena have shown, a mass movement to bring about fundamental transformation is potentially in the making, as long as the left can develop the tools and strategies necessary to bring about real change.

Thinking longer-term, a massive effort – on the scale of what the neoliberals have accomplished over four decades – is needed to lay down the institutional and policy foundations for advancing the elements of a coherent next system and a strategy for how to put them in place. The need for a major intervention at a greater scale is increasingly obvious. Efforts to cobble together solutions to today's challenges commonly draw upon the very same institutional arrangements and practices that gave rise to the problems in the first place. What is required is a self-conscious effort to face the fact that the system itself has to be changed and a different kind of political economy created – and to institutionalise this in a movement and politics capable of amplifying this message, and projecting the successes and future potential of a new approach to the economy.

Labour's Institutional Turn

Nowhere in the world is this ambitious and radical new economic agenda being developed more fully than in the United Kingdom, with the British Labour Party pushing forward a promising new agenda for economic change. For the first time in decades a radical agenda for systemic economic transformation is taking shape on the British left at the level of both ideas and practice. Offering real, on-the-ground solutions to communities and regions battered by successive waves of disinvestment, deindustrialisation, displacement, and disempowerment, it is based on a new configuration of institutions and approaches capable of producing more sustainable, lasting, and democratic outcomes. Rooted in place-based economics, democratic participation and control, and mobilising the untapped power of the local public sector, this emerging new political economy is also striking for being a transatlantic agenda – one that can find and is increasingly finding powerful application in both the United Kingdom under ambitious local authorities, and in the United States via the emboldened left politics of Bernie Sanders, Alexandria Ocasio-Cortez, and the Justice Democrats.

What's happening in Preston, and the advances on Community Wealth Building approaches that are taking shape, are now spurring excitement and a sense of possibility across the United Kingdom. There is an opportunity – in the unknown amount of time between now and the next UK general election – to familiarise people with the emerging new economic agenda through a widespread embrace of Community Wealth Building approaches by councils and local authorities, and shifting these ideas into the mainstream of broader economic policy, as is already taking place.

The 'institutional turn' in Labour's thinking under Jeremy Corbyn and John McDonnell is a direct response to the magnitude of the challenges now confronting the United Kingdom. More than half of all wealth is now held by the top 10 per cent, with around 20 per cent held by the top 1 per cent, and inequality continues to grow.[15] If we are serious about addressing real economic challenges then we need a different set of institutions and arrangements capable of producing sustainable, lasting, and more democratic outcomes.

The remarkable developments in the political and economic thinking of the Labour Party in recent years mean that it has moved to the point of advancing just such fundamental change. After a long period of straitened assumptions about economic policy during the years of neoliberal dominance, a space has now been opened up for a far broader political conversation on the economy than has been possible in decades. 'Co-operatives, shared ownership, and workplace democracy', John McDonnell has stated, 'all have a central role to play here' – 'here' being at the heart of what he terms 'the new economics'.[16] Corbyn, for his part, has promised 'decisive action to make finance the servant of industry not the masters of all', and called for local councils to be given more freedom to run utilities and services in order to 'roll back the tide of forced privatisation' and allow communities to shape and secure their economic futures.[17] Not since the 1970s and early 1980s – when the Labour Party was committed to bringing about what Tony Benn termed 'a fundamental and irreversible shift in the balance of power and wealth in favour of working people and their families' – has Labour put forward as bold a plan for the transformation of Britain.[18]

It can only be encouraging for the prospects of economic transformation in the UK that Labour is now charting a course beyond neoliberalism, advancing the elements of a vision of what would be involved in democratising the economy. Widely described as a (merely) social democratic programme, Labour's 2017 general election manifesto, *For the Many Not the Few*, in fact contains the seeds of a radical transformation beyond social democracy. Policies such as taking the major utilities, railways, and the postal service back into public hands, establishing a national investment fund to help 'rebuild communities ripped apart by globalisation', linking public sector procurement to a regionally balanced industrial strategy, creating a national investment bank and a network of new regional public banks in support of small and medium-sized enterprises, and democratising ownership by supporting co-ops and worker-owned firms, all represent a break with tired neoliberal orthodoxies. In combination with a commitment to devolving power and decision-making to local communities, and forming a Constitutional Convention that 'will look at extending democracy locally, regionally and nationally, considering the option of a more federalised country', the contours of a very different pattern of political economy begin to appear.

What is perhaps more striking even than this set of ambitions and commitments is that it can be seen as the beginning of a broader agenda of economic democracy. For Corbyn, McDonnell, and their aides, the manifesto is clearly a jumping off point and not the last word on economic change. A few days before the June 2017 election, Labour released *Alternative Models of Ownership*, a report to McDonnell and Rebecca Long-Bailey, Shadow Secretary of State for Business, Energy and Industrial Strategy, authored by a group of radical theorists and practitioners. This report presents the outlines of an exciting economic programme. It models the way in which the wider left should now be rolling up its sleeves and getting to work, going beyond rhetoric to detailed institutional design and policy formulation. In particular, the authors call on Labour to 'push issues of economic ownership and control to the front of the political agenda' and 'commence work on a strategy to win support' for such ideas – including an extensive programme of democratic public ownership, a policy framework conducive to the rapid growth of the cooperative sector, and a 'right to own' policy that would give workers the right of first refusal to buy their companies when they are up for sale or threatened with closure.[19]

There are huge potential benefits to pursuing a massive expansion of democratic ownership of enterprises. The opportunity presented by the coming 'silver tsunami' of retiring baby-boomer business owners, and the succession question this raises for large numbers of firms that might otherwise be wound down or gobbled up by private equity, means that the time for such an expansion is now. By one estimate, 400,000 such businesses could close in the next five years if the retiring owners are unable to find a buyer, putting between 2 and 4 million jobs at risk.[20] *For the Many Not the Few* called for a workers' 'right to own' principle and *Alternative Models of Ownership* takes this further, urging among other things that local authorities should be actively supporting and funding the incubation and expansion of worker co-ops and other social enterprises as part of their local economic development strategies – as is now happening in cities across the United States, as well as in Preston.[21] It also suggests that Labour should investigate the benefits and limitations of Employee Stock Ownership Plans (ESOPs), which – again as in the United States – could dramatically increase worker ownership with little risk or cost to workers.

In a political landscape fractured and divided by Brexit, decentralised public control of the economy could reconstitute the basis for democratic participation by giving people real decision-making power over the forces that affect their lives – a chance to actually 'take back control'. Meanwhile, debacles over outsourcing to Capita and Carillion, together with the long shadow cast by the Grenfell Tower fire disaster, underscore the importance of replacing an increasingly moribund neoliberal service-delivery model that appears to be very much on its last legs. The embrace of economic democracy in Labour's thinking seeks to replace such financialised economic forms with democratic alternatives of real benefit to ordinary people. This can begin right away, wherever the Party is in power at the local level, with no need to wait for a Labour government nationally – and the Community Wealth Building Unit was set up in 2018 in Corbyn's office for exactly this purpose.

Taken as a whole, the essential purpose of Labour's 'institutional turn' is to bring about an egalitarian rebalancing of power through a reordering of the basic institutions of the economy. The elements of the new political economy already under development will go a long way in this regard. However, much more remains to be done. The idea of a National Education Service clearly fits within such an approach, with cradle-to-grave access to education affording individuals opportunities for self-development independent of their economic means. The NES could be a transformative institution, as important to twenty-first-century democratic socialism in Britain as the NHS has been over the past seventy years. But clearly it is an idea in need of further elaboration, so as to design an institutional structure that could make good on such an ambitious promise.[22]

The NES points towards a broader agenda that asks what other kinds of social entitlements might be brought outside of the domain of the market and reimagined as elements of democratic citizenship. Recent work on Universal Basic Services suggests that there may be scope for providing a range of social services on a universal basis – from public transport to access to information via the internet – thereby increasing the size of the social sphere and the benefits of citizenship, whilst empowering individuals through reducing their dependence on market outcomes.[23]

Corbyn and McDonnell have created a hugely important opening for the left in Britain and beyond. Labour's institutional turn is bringing together the elements of what would amount to a transformational shift, broadening ownership, control, and participation, and promising a more egalitarian and democratic economy. Like the Attlee and Thatcher programmes before it, Corbynism contains the possibility of conjuring up the conditions for its own political success and consolidation. As such, it represents an opportunity for all on the left to support the development of a programme of fundamental change that is so urgently needed – and, in so doing, create a powerful model for emulation far and wide. The task is now to put further flesh on the bones of this transformative agenda in the face of the deep structural challenges of a fluid and rapidly changing political and economic landscape, thereby creating an economy that works 'for the many not the few'.

*

At a time of renewed crisis and uncertainty on both sides of the Atlantic, the outlines of a new economic paradigm are beginning to take shape. Community Wealth Building is where this next system begins. A powerful story is developing, beginning in Cleveland and Preston, that is seeing the growing effect that these models and others are having on policy and practice in an increasing number of cities across the United States and United Kingdom. The advances on Community Wealth Building approaches that are taking shape are creating a politically potent sense of excitement, possibility, and hope. They illuminate how new approaches can work in practice and generate new solutions to economic challenges. It is becoming possible to see how, by projecting and extending these practical experiments, the underlying structural building blocks of a new political-economic system might be assembled. There is a route beyond neoliberal crisis and decay, to take us to something better.

What is now needed is an integrated and strategic effort to bring all this together and to show how, in total, it forms the lineaments of a radically different system capable of delivering superior social, economic, and ecological outcomes. In this way we can aim to generate the fundamental transformation of our political economy that we so urgently need. As the long dark night of neoliberalism comes to a close, radical economic change appears once again to be within our grasp. That makes this the most exciting time to be active on the left in a generation.

Further Reading and Resources for Action

The Democracy Collaborative:
  https://democracycollaborative.org

Community Wealth Building:
  https://community-wealth.org

The Next System Project:
  https://thenextsystem.org

Centre for Local Economic Strategies (CLES):
  https://cles.org.uk

Common Wealth:
  https://common-wealth.co.uk/

IPPR Centre for Economic Justice:
  https://www.ippr.org/cej

New Economics Foundation (NEF):
  https://neweconomics.org/

New Economy Coalition:
  https://neweconomy.net

Transnational Institute:
  https://www.tni.org/en

Notes

Chapter 1

1 Marjorie Kelly and Ted Howard, *The Making of a Democratic Economy: Building Prosperity for the Many, Not Just the Few* (San Francisco: Berrett-Koehler, 2019), xv.

2 Steve Dubb, Ted Howard, and Sarah McKinley, 'Economic Democracy', in *Achieving Sustainability: Visions, Principles, and Practices* (2013), https://democracycollaborative.org/sites/clone.community-wealth.org/files/downloads/econ%20democracy.pdf.

3 George Eaton, 'How Preston – the UK's "Most Improved City" – Became a Success Story for Corbynomics', *New Statesman*, 1 November 2018, https://www.newstatesman.com/politics/uk/2018/11/how-preston-uk-s-most-improved-city-became-success-story-corbynomics.

4 PwC, *Good Growth for Cities* (2018); Richard

Partington, 'Preston Named as Most Improved City in UK', *Guardian*, 1 November 2018, https://www. theguardian.com/politics/2018/nov/01/preston-nam ed-as-most-most-improved-city-in-uk.

5 Chris Kahn, 'US Voters Want Leader to End Advantage of Rich and Powerful: Reuters/Ipsos Poll', 8 November 2016, www.reuters.com/article/us-usa-election-poll- mood-idUSKBN1332NC?il=0.

6 Resolution Foundation, *Are We Nearly There Yet? Spring Budget 2017 and the 15 Year Squeeze on Family and Public Finances* (March 2017), http:// www.resolutionfoundation.org/app/uploads/2017/ 03/Spring-Budget-2017-response.pdf.

7 See 'It's Time to Face the Depth of the Systemic Crisis We Confront: The Next System, A Call for National Discussion and Debate', The Next System Project, 31 March 2015, https://thenextsystem.org/download-the-next-system-project-statement-on-systemic-crisis.

8 The Next System Project's *Elements of the Democratic Economy* series maps this landscape of real-world practice, describing the institutions involved, assessing their transformative characteristics and potential, and providing examples and a sense of the challenges yet to be overcome (see https://thenext system.org/elements). See also Gar Alperovitz, *What Then Must We Do? Straight Talk About the Next American Revolution* (White River Junction: Chelsea Green, 2013); and Gar Alperovitz, *America Beyond Capitalism: Reclaiming Our Wealth, Our Liberty, and Our Democracy* (Takoma Park: Democracy Collaborative Press, 2011).

9 James Meade, *Efficiency, Equality and the Ownership of Property* (London: Routledge, 1964); Martin O'Neill and Stuart White, 'James Meade, Public Ownership, and the Idea of a Citizens' Trust', *International Journal of Public Policy* 15:1/2 (2019), 21–37.

10 Thomas Michael Power, *Lost Landscapes and Failed Economies* (Washington, DC: Island Press, 1996), 37.

11 Nick Wingfield and Patricia Cohen, 'Amazon Plans Second Headquarters, Opening a Bidding War Among Cities', *New York Times*, 7 September 2017, https://www.nytimes.com/2017/09/07/technology/amazon-headquarters-north-america.html.

12 Thad Williamson, David Imbroscio, and Gar Alperovitz, *Making a Place for Community: Local Democracy in a Global Era* (New York: Routledge, 2002), 56.

13 For an alternative approach to measuring the true costs and benefits to the public of private investment activity, see the notion of the 'local public balance sheet' in David Imbroscio, *Urban America Reconsidered: Alternatives for Governance and Policy* (Ithaca: Cornell University Press, 2010), chapter 5.

14 Marjorie Kelly, *Owning Our Future: The Emerging Ownership Revolution* (San Francisco: Berrett-Koehler, 2012), 19.

Chapter 2

1 Christine Berry and Joe Guinan, *People Get Ready! Preparing for a Corbyn Government* (London: O/R Books, 2019).

2 Joe Guinan and Martin O'Neill, 'The Institutional Turn: Labour's New Political Economy', *Renewal* 26:2 (2018), 5–16.

3 Centre for Local Economic Strategies, *Restoring Public Values in Public Services* (Manchester: CLES, 2018), 3.

4 Ibid., 8.

5 Matthew Brown and Martin O'Neill, 'The Road to Socialism is the A59: The Preston Model', *Renewal* 24:2 (2016), 69–78, at p. 73.; Aditya Chakrabortty, 'In 2011 Preston Hit Rock Bottom. Then It Took Back Control', *Guardian*, 31 January 2018. Tom Kibasi of IPPR describes Preston's approach to Community Wealth Building as 'a practical example of "taking back control"', in 'Jeremy Corbyn's Model Town', *The Economist*, 21 October 2017.

6 Labour Party, *Alternative Models of Ownership: Report to the Shadow Chancellor and the Shadow Secretary of State for Business, Energy and Industrial Strategy* (June 2017), https://labour.org.uk/wp-con tent/uploads/2017/10/Alternative-Models-of-Owner ship.pdf.

7 J. S. Mill, *The Principles of Political Economy*, Book IV, Chapter VIII, 'On the Probable Futurity of the Labouring Classes' (Oxford: Oxford University Press, 1994 [1848]). See also John Rawls,

Lectures on the History of Political Philosophy (Cambridge, MA: Harvard University Press, 2007), 249–316.

8 Mill, *The Principles of Political Economy*, Book V, Chapter XI, 'On the Ground and Limits of the Laissez-Fair or Non-Interference Principle', p. 334. See also Carole Pateman, *Participation and Democratic Theory* (Cambridge: Cambridge University Press, 1970), 22–44.

9 G. D. H. Cole, *Self-government in Industry* (London: G. Bell & Sons, 1919); *Social Theory* (London: Methuen, 1920); *Guild Socialism Restated* (London: Leonard Parsons, 1920); Pateman, *Participation and Democratic Theory*; Joshua Cohen, 'The Economic Basis of Deliberative Democracy', in Ellen Frankel Paul, Fred Miller, and Jeffrey Paul (eds), *Socialism* (Oxford: Blackwell, 1989), 25–50. See also Martin O'Neill, 'Three Rawlsian Routes Towards Economic Democracy', *Revue de Philosophie Économique* 9:1 (2008), 29–55.

10 Cohen, 'The Economic Basis of Deliberative Democracy', 29.

11 Emily McTernan et al., 'If You Care About Social Equality, You Want a Big State: Home, Work, Care and Social Egalitarianism', *Juncture* 23:2 (2016), 138–44; Martin O'Neill, 'Creating a More Equal Future', in Andrew Harrop and Ed Wallis (eds), *Future Left* (London: Fabian Society, 2016).

12 Anna Bawden, 'Why Councils are Bringing Millions of Pounds Worth of Services Back In-House', *Guardian*, 29 May 2019, https://www.theguardian.

com/society/2019/may/29/bringing-services-back-in-house-is-good-councils.

13 Joe Guinan and Thomas M. Hanna, 'Democratic Ownership in the New Economy', in John McDonnell (ed.), *Economics for the Many* (London: Verso, 2018), 108–25.

14 Martin O'Neill and Thad Williamson (eds), *Property-Owning Democracy: Rawls and Beyond* (Hoboken: Wiley-Blackwell, 2012).

15 Williamson et al., *Making a Place for Community*.

16 Martin O'Neill, 'Philosophy and Public Policy after Piketty', *Journal of Political Philosophy* 25:3 (2017), 343–75.

17 O'Neill, 'Three Rawlsian Routes towards Economic Democracy'; Martin O'Neill, 'What Should Egalitarians Believe?', *Philosophy & Public Affairs* 36:2 (2008), 119–56.

18 On the importance of shared, public institutions, see Bonnie Honig, *Public Things: Democracy in Disrepair* (New York: Fordham University Press, 2017).

19 On neoliberalism as the coercive imposition of market-type competition in areas outside the market, see William Davies, *The Limits of Neoliberalism: Authority, Sovereignty and the Logic of Competition*, revised edition (London: SAGE, 2016).

20 Derek Parfit, *On What Matters*, Vol. 1 (Oxford: Oxford University Press, 2011), chapter 13, 'What If Everyone Did That?' See also Derek Parfit, *Reasons and Persons* (Oxford: Oxford University Press, 1984), Part One.

21 For a clarifying introduction to the economic case against protectionism, see Mathias Risse, 'Fairness in Trade I: Obligations from Trading and the Pauper-Labor Argument', *Philosophy, Politics and Economics* 6:3 (2007), 355–77.

22 Kibasi, 'Jeremy Corbyn's Model Town'.

23 'Corbynomics: The Great Transformation', *The Economist*, 19 May 2018.

24 See Thomas Piketty's discussion of the growth of the capital share of national income, and the fall of the labour share, since the period of *Les Trentes Glorieuses*, in his *Capital in the Twenty-First Century* (Cambridge, MA: Harvard University Press, 2014). See also O'Neill, 'Philosophy and Public Policy After Piketty'.

25 See Daniel Hausmann, Michael McPherson, and Debra Satz, *Economic Analysis, Moral Philosophy and Public Policy*, 3rd edition (Cambridge: Cambridge University Press, 2017), chapter 9; see also John Quiggin, *Economics in Two Lessons* (Princeton: Princeton University Press, 2019), chapter 7.

26 See Jonathan Wolff, 'Making the World Safe for Utilitarianism', *Royal Institute of Philosophy Supplement* 58 (2006), 1–22.

27 See Nicholas Kaldor, 'Welfare Propositions of Economics and Interpersonal Comparisons of Utility', *Economic Journal* 49 (1939), 549–52; and John Hicks, 'The Foundations of Welfare Economics', *Economic Journal* 49 (1939): 696–712.

28 With thanks to Leah Downey and Marco Meyer for discussion of ideas of economic efficiency.

29 Williamson et al., *Making a Place for Community*, 9.

30 See Ha-Joon Chang, *Kicking Away the Ladder: Development Strategy in Historical Perspective* (London: Anthem Press, 2003); *Bad Samaritans: The Myth of Free Trade and the Secret History of Capitalism* (London: Bloomsbury, 2007); *23 Things They Don't Tell You About Capitalism* (London: Bloomsbury, 2010).

31 Ted Howard and Martin O'Neill, 'Beyond Extraction: The Case for Community Wealth Building', *Renewal* 26:2 (2018), 46–53.

32 On social justice and corporate tax avoidance, see Martin O'Neill, 'The Social Injustice of Corporate Tax Avoidance', in John Christensen and Dan Hind (eds), *The Greatest Invention: Tax and the Campaign for a Just Society* (Margate: Commonwealth Publishing, 2015), 146–53.

33 'Corbynomics: The Great Transformation', *The Economist*, 19 May 2018.

34 Aditya Chakrabortty, 'Some Call It Outsourcing. I Call It Spivvery', *Guardian*, 23 April 2018, https://www.theguardian.com/commentisfree/2018/apr/23/capita-carillion-outsourcing-local-elections-aditya-chakrabortty.

35 Oscar Wilde, 'The Soul of Man Under Socialism' (1891), in *The Soul of Man Under Socialism and Selected Critical Prose*, ed. Linda Dowling, new edition (Harmondsworth: Penguin Books, 2001).

36 Authors' visit to Mondragón, May 2018. See also Ander Etxeberria and Martin O'Neill, 'On Mondragon – Solidarity, Democracy, and the Value

of Work: An Interview with Ander Etxeberria',
Renewal, 19 July 2019, http://www.renewal.org.uk/
blog/on-mondragon-solidarity-democracy-value-of-
work.

Chapter 3

1 Joe Guinan and Thomas M. Hanna, 'Polanyi Against
the Whirlwind', *Renewal* 25:1 (2017), 5–12.
2 Robert Dahl, *A Preface to Economic Democracy*
(Berkeley: University of California Press, 1986), 4.
3 Cole, *Guild Socialism Re-stated*, 12.
4 Piketty, *Capital in the Twenty-First Century*; O'Neill,
'Philosophy and Public Policy After Piketty'.
5 Joe Guinan, 'Social Democracy in the Age of
Austerity and Resistance: The Radical Potential
of Democratising Capital', *Renewal* 20:4 (2012),
9–19.
6 See André Gorz, *Strategy for Labor: A Radical
Proposal* (Boston: Beacon Press, 1967).
7 See Joe Guinan and Thomas M. Hanna, 'Full
Corbynism: Constructing a New Left Political
Economy Beyond Neoliberalism', *New Socialist*, 19
June 2019, https://newsocialist.org.uk/full-corbyn
ism-constructing-a-new-left-political-economy-bey
ond-neoliberalism.
8 Satoko Kishimoto and Oliver Petijean, *Reclaiming
Public Services: How Cities and Citizens are
Turning Back Privatisation* (Amsterdam and Paris:
Transnational Institute, 2017), https://www.tni.org/

files/publication-downloads/reclaiming_public_servi
ces.pdf.

9 See Chang, *23 Things They Don't Tell You About Capitalism*, especially Thing 19.

10 See the Participatory Budgeting Project, https://www. participatorybudgeting.org.

11 Rowland Atkinson, 'London's Emptying Towers', *Le Monde Diplomatique*, March 2018, https://monded iplo.com/2018/03/03brexit-london-homeless.

12 Niki Seth-Smith, 'In the Western Isles', LRB Blog, 6 February 2014, https://www.lrb.co.uk/blog/2014/ february/in-the-western-isles; John Emmeus Davis, *The Community Land Trust Reader* (Cambridge, MA: Lincoln Institute of Land Policy, 2010); Helmut Gruber, *Red Vienna: Experiment in Working Class Culture 1919–1934* (Oxford: Oxford University Press, 1991); Quintin Bradley, *The Tenants' Movement: Resident Involvement, Community Action, and the Contentious Politics of Housing* (New York: Routledge, 2014).

13 Michael Foot, *Aneurin Bevan: A Biography, Volume Two: 1945–1960* (New York: Atheneum, 1974), 106.

14 See Hilary Wainwright, *A New Politics from the Left* (Cambridge: Polity, 2018), 133, n. 14.

15 For UK inequality data, see the World Inequality Database, http://wid.world/country/united-kingdom.

16 John McDonnell, Speech at Co-op Ways Forward Conference, Co-operative Party, 21 January 2016, https://party.coop/2016/01/21/john-mcdonnell-spee ch-at-co-op-ways-forward-conference.

17 Jeremy Corbyn, 'We Will Make Finance the Servants of Industry', 20 February 2018, https://labour.org.uk/press/will-make-finance-servants-industry-jeremy-corbyn.

18 On Labour's Alternative Economic Strategy in the 1970s, see John Medhurst, *That Option No Longer Exists: Britain 1974–76* (Alresford: Zero Books, 2014), and Mark Wickham-Jones, *Economic Strategy and the Labour Party: Politics and Policy-Making, 1970–83* (Basingstoke: Palgrave Macmillan, 1996). See also Stuart Holland, *The Socialist Challenge* (London: Quartet Books, 1976). For a recent interview with Holland, see Stuart Holland and Martin O'Neill, 'Hope Amidst Despair? Stuart Holland on Brexit, Europe and Labour's New Economics', *Renewal* 25:3–4 (2017), 90–100.

19 Labour Party, *Alternative Models of Ownership*, 32.

20 Alexandra Frean, 'Baby-boomer Business Owners Must Be Ready to Hand Over the Reins', *The Times*, 19 July 2017.

21 Marjorie Kelly, Sarah McKinley and Violeta Duncan, 'Community Wealth Building: America's Emerging Asset-based Approach to City Economic Development', *Renewal* 24:2 (2016), 51–68.

22 Labour Party National Policy Forum, *Early Years, Education and Skills: Towards a National Education Service* (2018), https://www.policyforum.labour.org.uk/commissions/towards-a-national-education-service; Martin O'Neill and Liam Shields, 'Equality of Opportunity and State Education', *The Philosophers' Magazine* (7 June 2017), http://www.philosopher

smag.com/opinion/165-equality-of-opportunity-and-education-policy.

23 For a recent proposal on Universal Basic Services, see Jonathan Portes, Howard Reed, and Andrew Percy, *Social Prosperity for the Future: The Case for Universal Basic Services*, a Social Prosperity Network Report (London: UCL Institute for Global Prosperity, 2017), https://www.ucl.ac.uk/bartlett/igp/news/2017/oct/igps-social-prosperity-network-publishes-uks-first-report-universal-basic-services.

Index

absentee ownership 30, 84
affordable housing 12, 24,
     27, 92
'after the fact' intervention
     and redistribution 6, 29,
     32, 34, 90
Alaska 92, 103
Alperovitz, Gar x, 72
Amazon 29
anchor institutions 11, 12,
     25–6, 28, 48, 92
  economic footprint 11,
     15, 26, 48
  local authorities, working
     with 53
  procurement strategies 2,
     11, 95
Association for Public Service
     Excellence (APSE)
     52
Attlee government 104,
     114
austerity 3, 6, 27, 43
automation 89

banking
  credit unions 25
  crises 31, 105
  nationalising 94
  public/state and
     community 2, 3, 13, 26,
     89, 92, 110
Benn, Tony 109
Bevan, Nye 104
Brexit 60, 112
Brown, Matthew xi, 12,
     44–5
budgeting, participatory 92,
     100–1
buy-local strategies 30, 59
  see also municipal
     protectionism

California 103
Capita 77, 112
capital
  capital flight 10
  capital flows 99
  de-globalisation of 28

Index

institutional relationships 33
labour over capital 8, 45, 84
ownership and control of 87, 89
returns to capital 89
rooting in place 27
Carillion 77, 112
Centre for Local Economic Strategies (CLES) 12, 40
Chang, Ha-Joon 74
citizens' trusts 27
City of London 94
civil rights movement 24
Cleveland 18
Cleveland Model x, 10–12
climate change 85, 86, 97, 100
Cohen, Joshua 50, 62
Cole, G. D. H. 50, 88
collaborative decision-making 30
collective asset ownership 8, 27, 98
commons-based approach 27, 101, 102
community development corporations (CDCs) 24
community development financial institutions (CDFIs) 2, 24–5
community economic development
  alternative models see Community Wealth Building; economic democracy
  conventional model 29–31

community land trusts (CLTs) 2, 24, 28, 48, 89, 92, 102
Community Wealth Building ix
  critiques and counter-objections 38–9, 56–80
  democratic argument for 47–51
  flagship models see Cleveland Model; Preston Model
  institutional turn and 38, 79, 81–116
  justifications for 36–55
  main principles and values of 2–3, 5–9, 10, 37–8, 39–40, 84–5
  non-material benefits 60, 61–3
  origins of 9, 17–23
  see also systemic change
community-sustaining policies 22, 96, 102
Cooperative Home Care Associates (CHCA) 25
cooperatives 25, 28, 89, 92, 98, 108, 110
  platform cooperatives 92
  worker cooperatives 3, 11, 25, 28, 89, 92, 94–5, 96, 97, 110
Corbyn, Jeremy 81, 105, 108–9, 110, 114
Corbynomics 59, 114
  see also UK Labour Party
corporate subsidies
  expiry of 31
  race to the bottom 29

Index

corporations
  community corporations
    28
  corporate capture 77
  corporate leverage 22,
    23, 28
  corporate social
    responsibility 41
  corporate subsidies 29, 31
  corporate tax avoidance
    75
  locational blackmail 22,
    29
  multinational 2, 12, 52,
    75, 95
  nonprofit 10, 11, 24
  public ownership of 97
  restructurings 18, 34
credit unions 25
cronyism 76

Dahl, Robert 88
decommodification 27, 102
deindustrialisation 1, 10, 18,
  31, 99, 107
Deliveroo 92
democracy
  active citizenship 48, 49,
    50, 51, 54
  equality and democracy,
    mutually reinforcing
    53–5, 80
  extending 46–51, 54–5,
    110
  neoliberal impact on 47
  political and economic
    democratic relations
    49–50
Democracy Collaborative
  ix–x, 7, 9, 11, 24

democratised economy see
  economic democracy
Detroit 18, 31
disempowerment 1, 46–7,
  85, 107
disinvestment 1, 10, 85, 99,
  107
displacement 1, 23, 24, 107
distributive considerations
  64, 66, 68, 69, 70
  see also redistribution
Dubb, Steve 9

Each-We Dilemma 58
Eaton, George 13
ecological collapse 86
economic democracy 2, 3, 6,
  8, 15, 28–9, 44, 44–6,
  83–7, 88–91
  citizen engagement 78–80
  core ideas of 9–10, 88
  emerging mosaic of 23–31
  experimentation 91–3
  precondition for a
    democratic society
    49–50
  systemic change and 83–7,
    93–102, 105, 106
  'Wildean' line of critique
    78
economic efficiency 61, 62,
  64, 65, 66–70
  Kaldor-Hicks efficiency 68
  Pareto efficiency 67–8
  technical concept of 66–7
economic inequality see
  income and wealth
  inequalities
economic stagnation 17,
  33, 85

Index

economic system change *see* systemic change

economic waste 73

elite ownership 2, 8, 30

emerging social movements 105

Employee Stock Ownership Plans (ESOPs) 25, 112

employees *see* workers

environmental destruction 23, 34, 82, 85, 86

Evergreen Cooperatives, Cleveland 10, 11, 12

extractive economy 2, 8, 12, 27, 33, 52, 53, 74–5

far right 22, 83, 87
  populism 99

financialisation 31, 34, 94, 101, 112

free trade agreements 99

Gateshead 42

Gross Domestic Product (GDP) 21

gentrification 24, 27, 92

geopolitical power 21

Gorz, André 93

Great Depression 103

Great Financial Crisis 31

green manufacturing strategies and services 95, 96

Green New Deal 95, 96

Grenfell Tower fire disaster 112

guild socialism 50

Hicks, John 68

Hock, Dee Ward 87

hospitals 3, 25, 26, 48
  see also anchor institutions

housing
  affordable 12, 24, 27, 92
  decommodification of 101
  democratising ownership of 102

Howard, Ted x, 7, 9

Imbroscio, David 72

income and wealth inequalities 8, 19, 20, 21, 23, 30, 85, 108

industrial strategy 95–6, 109

institutional turn 38, 79, 81–116

Justice Democrats 107

Kaldor, Nicholas 68

Kaldor-Hicks efficiency 68, 70

Kelly, Marjorie x–xi, 7, 33

Keynesian economics 32, 34

laboratories of democracy ix, 6, 16, 22, 86, 102

labour arbitrage 33

labour movements 32, 34

labour over capital 8, 45, 84

laissez-faire ideology 103

land
  community buyouts of 102
  community land trusts 2, 24, 28, 48, 89, 92, 102
  decommodification of 101
  democratising ownership of 27, 92, 102

Index

the left, strategically minded
35, 98–9, 105
see also UK Labour Party
libertarian socialism 9
living wage policies 30, 52
local authorities *see* local
    public sector
local justice ix, 44
local multipliers 27, 30, 74,
84, 95
local public sector
   anchor institutions,
    working with 53
   austerity policies 43
   bringing back services in-
    house 52
   cost-driven policies 40, 41,
    43, 44, 56, 66
   economic footprint 22–3
   economically activist
    model 41–2, 43, 44–6,
    53, 56
   outsourcing 2, 3, 41,
    61–2, 65, 66, 68, 69,
    77, 112
   political values 39, 40
   shaping the economic and
    social landscape 41–2,
    43, 44–6, 56
   social care provision 41,
    42–3
Long-Bailey, Rebecca 110

McDonnell, John 81, 108,
110, 114
McInroy, Neil 12
McKinley, Sarah xiv, 9
market forces 103
mass political parties 34
Meade, James 27

Mill, John Stuart 49, 62
Mondragón 45, 79
municipal protectionism
57–75
mutual and credit unions 94

National Education Service
(NES) 113
National Health Service
(NHS) 15, 104, 113
national investment fund
109
nationalisation 94, 100
neoliberalism ix, 32
   accommodation to 33
   case against Community
    Wealth Building 71–5
   Clinton era 18
   democratic decision-
    making, suppression
    of 47
   displacing 29
   economic model 7, 8, 12,
    16, 17, 27, 37, 56
   employment practices 53
   failed model of 7, 9, 16,
    34, 82, 110
   idealised version of 77
   impersonal logic of the
    market 47, 49
   passive consumer model
    of 84
New Public Management
39–40
non-material benefits of
   Community Wealth
   Building 61–3, 64
   justifiable costs 61, 63
North American Free Trade
   Agreement (NAFTA) 18

Index

Ocasio-Cortez, Alexandria
107
offshoring 28, 34, 99
O'Neill, Tip viii
outsourcing 2, 3, 41, 61–2,
66, 68, 69, 77, 112
ownership
broadening and
democratising 10, 27,
48, 84, 89, 92, 94–5,
102, 110–11, 111
capitalist private
ownership 87
worker ownership 3, 11,
25, 28, 89, 92, 94–5, 96,
97, 110

Pareto efficiency 67–8, 70
Parfit, Derek 58
Pateman, Carole 50, 62
peak globalisation 98
pension funds 12, 18
community development
and 26
permanent normal trade
relations (PNTR) 19
Piketty, Thomas 89
place
embedded costs of 72–3
place-based economics and
politics 1, 3, 8, 10, 30,
73, 82, 84, 95, 107
planning
participatory 92–3, 96,
99–100, 101
regional economic
planning 95
planning commissions
101
Polanyi, Karl 86–7

political radicalism, emerging
7, 105, 106–7
popular sovereignty 10
populism 99
post-industrial decline 95
postwar settlement 33, 104
institutional underpinnings
of 32, 34
poverty 18, 31, 97
place- and race-based 23
Preston Model xi, 12–13,
14, 15, 58, 83, 107
PricewaterhouseCoopers 14
Prisoner's Dilemma 58
privatisation of public
services 3, 97, 109
property speculation 27, 92,
101
protectionism 74, 99
municipal protectionism
58–9, 75
public sector
economic development
programmes 26–7, 84,
112
expanded and reimagined
97
procurement policies 109
top-down centralised
model 97
utilities 26, 109
see also local public sector
public-private partnerships 2
public–public partnerships
98

racial and gender disparities
85
re-circulatory local
economies 3, 27, 84, 95

Index

real estate bubbles 27, 92
reconstruction, politics of 16
redistribution 6, 29, 34, 38, 60, 68, 69, 70, 88, 90
remunicipalisation 98
renationalisation 109
rent extraction 57, 76, 77
rentier finance 3, 94
rustbelt cities 17–18, 19, 31
  see also Cleveland; Detroit

Sanders, Bernie 105, 107
service-delivery model, neoliberal 112
shareholder value, pursuit of 18, 31
sharing economy 92
social atomisation 34, 85
social care provision 41, 42–3
  low-cost 42, 43
  respect for clients and providers 43
social democracy 87–9, 90, 91
social and economic crisis 5, 17–22, 24, 33
social and economic equality 37, 51–3, 54
  equality and democracy, close relations between 53–5, 80
social justice viii, x, 3, 36, 37, 56
Social Value Act 2012 40, 76
socialised medicine 104
Solow, Robert 89
state socialism 87
stewardship 8, 102

sustainability 8, 95
systemic change x, 3, 6, 16, 29, 30, 35, 83–7, 106
  pathways to 93–102, 105
systemic crisis 82, 85, 90

Talbot, Colin 59
taxation 90
  corporate tax avoidance 75
  tax incentives, locational 2, 30
  'tax and spend' transfer policies 88
tenants' movement 102
Texas 92
'throw-away cities' phenomenon 31, 73
tick-box exercises 41
Tithebarn project 12
trade
  liberalisation 18
  protectionism 99
  reconceptualised trade model 98–9
trade unions 91
Tredegar Medical Aid Society 104
trickle down economics 30, 84
Trump, Donald 19–20, 99
trusts
  citizens' trusts 27
  community land trusts 2, 24, 28, 48, 89, 92, 102
  public 27, 92

Uber 92
UK Labour Party 76, 81, 83
  2017 general election manifesto 109, 110

Index

Community Wealth
  Building Unit xiii, 15,
  113
  institutional turn 81, 83,
  106–16
United Kingdom ix
  economic disparities 20,
  108
  left politics 106–7
  new dynamic 14–15
  Preston Model xi, 12–13,
  14, 15, 58, 83, 107
  see also UK Labour Party
United States ix, 7
  American liberalism 91
  Cleveland Model x,
  10–12
  Clinton era 19
  economic inequality 19
  left politics 107
  New Deal 102–3
  new dynamic 7, 14, 24–7
  Obama economy 19
  social and economic crisis
  17–20, 24
  social security system 103
  see also Democracy
  Collaborative
Universal Basic Services
  113–14
universities 25, 26, 48
  see also anchor institutions
utilities 26, 109

wage stagnation 17, 20, 66
Wall Street 94
Wall Street Crash 103

wealth
  democratisation of 28,
  89–90
  inequalities 8, 19, 20, 21,
  23, 30, 85, 108
wealth tax 89
Wilde, Oscar 78
Williamson, Thad 72
workers
  business ownership 3, 11,
  25, 28, 89, 92, 94–5, 96,
  97, 110
  cooperatives 2, 10, 11, 25,
  48, 95, 112
  dignified and secure
  employment, right to
  42, 53, 65–6
  long-term investment in
  72
  poor employment
  conditions 53, 62
  'right to own' policy
  111–12
  skills and development 30,
  72, 96
  supposedly 'new' jobs 29,
  31
  workers-as-citizens 65,
  70, 71
  workers-as-costs 65, 70,
  71, 72

xenophobic nationalism 83

zero-hour contracts 42, 53,
  61
zero-sum game 29, 58, 60